FATHER JOE

SOUTHIE WILL NEVER FORGET YOU

THE GIFT OF LOVE IS GIVING LOVE TO OTHERS
W. THOMAS STAFFORD

DEDICATION

To my wife Emma, thank you for helping me tell the story of Father Joseph Laporte. I could not have accomplished it without you.

To my daughter Kathleen, your Master's degree in communication revealed itself during all of your proof-reading and editing.

To my daughter Susan, thank you for all of your IT skills which helped immensely.

To my daughters Karen and Kelly, thank you for all of your support and encouragement to never give up.

To all the men and women who are considering a religious life in any denomination: that they may be inspired by the example set by Father Joseph Laporte.

TABLE OF CONTENTS

Father Joe

PREFACE

The people you remember in your life are the ones who influenced you and helped you change course for the better.

For me, and many others in South Boston, Massachusetts, that person was Father Joseph E. Laporte. Father Joe, as we affectionately called him, was inspirational to all who knew him, including his fellow priests and more significantly to the people of South Boston. During the 1960's he was a parish priest for the families of St. Monica's and Gate of Heaven parishes; he celebrated Mass, administered the sacraments, prayed with the sick, comforted the broken-hearted. He was a counselor for families in need, a big brother for many and a father figure for some. He spent only six years as a curate before he died at the young age of 32 and yet in that short time, he left a profound effect on the South Boston community. His spiritual works inspired the residents to raise more than $10,000 to erect a statue in his honor, which still stands across from the Curley Center, formerly the L Street Bathhouse.

I left South Boston to join the United States Marine Corps in 1968 and was honorably discharged in 1971. I was unable to secure a law enforcement position in Boston. I was concerned that if I returned to Southie I would end up back in a gang and hanging out on the corners. I explored other options and found a job in New Jersey as a police officer. I have lived in New Jersey for more than 50 years and often go back with my family to visit Southie to recount the days of my youth. Our trips always include a stop at Father Laporte's statue. It recently occurred to me that many of the people living in South Boston, who have passed the statue multiple times, probably have no idea who the priest was, why the young lad was standing with him, or more importantly, how the statue was erected and what it represents. I was worried that soon there would be no one left to tell his story. That is what inspired me to write this memoir of the man who changed my life and the lives of many others almost 60 years ago. I wondered, where do I start? I received the invitation for my 50th high school reunion from South Boston High and I decided that may be a good place to begin. During that event I had an opportunity to announce my intention to draft a book about Father Laporte and requested if anyone had any memories of him, that they complete the questionnaire I supplied or just leave their name and contact information. To my surprise, I only received one response. It was from Joanne Derrah, my former classmate, who said that she thinks her brother may have some remembrances. That contact led me to 6 guys who were very close friends with Father Joe and were willing to share their stories. This core group agreed to meet at Amrheins Restaurant in Southie in 2019 and that was the birth of this book. In support of the project, the editor of South Boston Today offered to run the open letter that I wrote to the residents of South Boston for several months asking for their remembrances. I have learned many things in writing this book, not the least of which is that I should have started this venture long ago. In the more than 57 years since his death, many who knew him have died, memories have faded, and yet there are a few of us left who want to recount his story so his work is never forgotten. Father Joe never forgot us and we, in turn, want his legacy to go on forever. That is the essence of this book.

Though not my original intention, my research has led me to a loftier goal than writing this memoir. After talking to those who remember Father Joe, reading and re-reading their personal accounts, researching multiple newspaper articles at the Boston Public Library and examining the writings of Richard Cardinal Cushing, the bishops, the pastors, fellow priests, nuns and community leaders of the day, it occurred to me that Father Joe was more than an influence on me and the South Boston community. He was truly a 'servant of God', who walked among us while on this earth. Everyone who knew him would probably agree that he has been granted a special place in heaven. I propose that this memoir be a step towards Father Joe being named a 'Servant of God', which is the Catholic Church's first step towards canonization. I ask that if you are reading this book and have any knowledge, an eyewitness account, remember words from his sermons, have a note from Father Joe, a copy of his writings, a speech or homily you remember, you can be a significant part of this process. Please share with me at *fatherjoebook68@gmail.com*.

They say, "You can take the boy out of Southie, but you can't take the Southie out of the boy." These words keep resounding in my head, "If not me, who?? If not now, when??"

EARLY LIFE OF JOSEPH LAPORTE

His life starts at Saint Mary's Infant Asylum Hospital, a home for unwed mothers in Boston, Massachusetts, where a boy named Joseph Francis Hill was born on September 15, 1932. His mother cared for him for approximately three years, and then for unknown reasons, she allowed the adoption of her son to his biological father, Joseph Edward Laporte. He was their only child and spent his childhood in Haverhill, Massachusetts. I have reason to believe that Joe was baptized at St. Mary's Infant Asylum Hospital two days after his birth, on September 17, 1932. He received his Communion and Confirmation at Saint James Church in Haverhill and attended both the parish elementary and high schools. His first Holy Communion was on May 26, 1940, officiated by Father Joseph F. Sullivan. His Confirmation was officiated by Archbishop Richard Cardinal Cushing on June 2, 1945, and he chose the name Michael as his confirmation name.

While researching this book, I was able to locate and personally interview two family members of Joseph Laporte. I learned about his early childhood from two first cousins, Mrs. Norma Williams Riley and Mr. Humphrey Williams. During our conversations Norma, who was 18 months older than Joe, stated that she had four brothers and was in fragile health as a young girl. Her parents were concerned that she may catch tuberculosis, so they decided to send her to live with her cousin Joe and his family, to keep her safe and healthy. Norma lived with Joe from the age of seven to twelve years old. During these five years she would frequently return to her home to see her parents and four brothers. More than anyone in their family, she spent the most time with Joe. Together they shared a love and passion for dancing and became a professional dance team known as *Norma and Joe*. They routinely performed at school events, community gatherings and the USO.

Norma and Joe

Norma recalls one of the most memorable performances was when they entertained General George S. Patton and his family. When they were not performing professionally, as *Norma and Joe*, they would just enjoy practicing together. They would also entertain their schoolmates by walking home from school on their hands! Joe preferred dancing to studying and Norma remembers the day a nun told him, "Joe, all of your brains are in your feet!" Norma talked about Joe's love of music and how he had studied the piano and became good enough to play the organ at Saint James Church.

She described him as having a great sense of humor, as he was a real jokester and always enjoyed making everyone laugh. Norma recalls one day Joe's mother asked her to go to the store to buy toilet paper. She thought, "No way, it's too embarrassing I don't want to go". Joe said, "Come on, I'll go with you". They walked to the store, he bought the toilet paper and as they began to walk home Joe unwrapped one of the rolls. It was very windy that day and suddenly, Norma noticed there was a trail of toilet paper floating in the air behind them. Well, you can just imagine what that looked like. "Joe knew it would make me blush and embarrassed, but it was all in fun," said Norma.

As a youngster, Joe had some close calls with death, though obviously God had other plans for him. Norma credits herself with rescuing him from several dangerous situations. In one instance, there was a swampy marsh near the beach they frequented and a little water way that ran through it. As told by Norma, "We were quite young, seven or eight years old at the time. Joe had a yellow slicker jacket and he said, 'I'm putting it on backwards so buckle me up in the back'. Norma said she buckled his yellow slicker backwards, and he immediately ran into the marsh. She did not dare to run out with him because she had on her patent leather shoes and her aunt would be mad at her. "As I am watching him running out into the marsh he falls into the swamp and disappeared. I then ran out into the marsh and when I found him, he had fallen face down and wasn't moving. His slicker was on backwards and buckled in the back, so he did not have use of his arms. I lifted Joe up by his shoulders and pulled him up out of the swampy marsh, it was a very scary moment in our lives."

Norma described another incident in Joe's life that was a close call with death. She and Joe were at the beach on a stormy day with thunder and lightning. Joe had previously broken his arm which was secured in a sling. While they were running on the beach, suddenly lightning hit the large safety pin that held his sling together. The lightning singed that area but did not penetrate his skin.

Humphrey Williams, also a first cousin, was born and raised in Haverhill, MA, is a United States Navy Veteran, and former Haverhill City official. He had socialized frequently with Joe during his early life and recalls another incident that could have taken Joe's life. Joe and their friends would go swimming down to a place called, 'The Pipes' near the 'Little River.' This swimming area was behind Saint James Cemetery where there was a big sewer pipe running across the river. It happened that the City of Haverhill had put up barbed wire to prevent the kids from swimming at this location. However, one day the kids cut the wire and threw it into the river. At the same time Joe fell backwards into the water and onto the barbed wire. He was tangled up in it and there were cuts and blood all over his body. Humphrey still wonders to this day how Joe came out of that incident not seriously injured.

Humphrey stated, "I guess God had a plan for him."

Humphrey confirmed that both Norma and Joe were very talented dancers and shared their skills with everyone. He recalled them dancing at a local orphanage near Newburyport, MA and even years later, when driving by that location he can still see Joe standing out in front of the building.

Joseph Laporte (center) and Norma (top left) and other dancers

Joe's decision to enter the seminary was a moment in Norma's life she will never forget. She remembers him saying he wanted to talk to her. He picked her up in his mother's car and drove her up to "Mt. Washington," a hilly section of Haverhill, and stopped the car. He said to Norma, "I am going into the seminary to become a priest." The news surprised her.

How shocked she was at that moment! Norma said to him that it's an awful big decision to make right out of high school. She asked him if he was sure he did not want to go on to college. Norma said that he told her, "No! that's what I want to do." Norma did not recall feeling happy or unhappy. She knew that he had given it a lot of thought and that if it didn't work, he would not stay. She had mixed feelings, happy for him but sad that he would never live back in Haverhill.

Norma recalls his mother, now a widow, had initially tried to talk him out of it. She offered to turn all her property over to him for financial security. She also reminded him that if he became a priest he would never be married and have his own children. Over time, Joe's mother could see how strong his call was to the priesthood. She realized that neither she nor anyone could change his mind to follow his calling. She loved him so much and gave him her blessing to become a priest.

Both cousins believe what motivated him to become a priest was his years of Catholic education and the influence of several priests, including: Father Finn, Father Leo Dwyer, Father Madden (a cousin to Joe on his mother's side) and Bishop Minahan, all who had personal contact with Joe during his early life.

Before Joe entered the seminary, the family decided to tell him that he was adopted. Humphrey, who was in the Navy serving in Europe, said he heard from the family that when Joe heard the well-kept secret, he was so overwhelmed that he collapsed to the ground in Washington Square in downtown Haverhill.

Norma recalled Joe's family asking him if he wanted to

meet his biological mother. If so, they would set up a meeting. He responded, "No! My mother is my mother, I don't want another one."

He answered his calling to the priesthood by first attending Cardinal O'Connell (minor) Seminary before continuing his studies at Saint John Seminary, in Brighton, Massachusetts.

Humphrey remembers that sometime in 1952 or 1953 while on leave from the Navy, he visited the seminary several times to see Joe. He would buy Hoodsies (an ice cream cup) and candy bars, sneak into the seminary and hand them out to many of the seminarians. He went on to say that many men entered the seminary because of the Korean War and when the War ended in 1953, half of Joe's class left the seminary.

Father Laporte celebrating his first Mass

Southie Will Never Forget You

He was ordained by Richard Cardinal Cushing at the Cathedral of the Holy Cross on February 2, 1959. On February 16, 1959, Cardinal Cushing assigned him to St. Monica's Parish in South Boston and told him to "*look after its youth.*"

He celebrated his first mass in his home parish, Saint James, Haverhill, and Bishop Jeremiah F. Minihan preached at this mass.

Father Joe holding Humphrey Williams III, Arthur Bower (his cousins), and Father Madden

Norma recalls after that mass Father Joe was giving his blessings to young children. She reminded him that she had a one-year-old at home and had just delivered her second child. He told her that her next babies would be twins. It came to pass that eight months later his prediction came true, and she had twins! The next time she saw him was when he came to see her at the hospital after delivering her babies. She reminded him of what he had said to her eight months previously and joked that one of her twins was going back with him to South Boston!

Humphrey talked about how very sick his mother was (Father Joe's aunt) and asked Father Joe to pray for her. The next time Father Joe came to Haverhill, he gave her two relics of saints to pray to, Saint Aloysius and Saint John Berchmans. Since his mom's death, Humphrey is still in possession of these relics along with Father Joe's crucifix. He cherishes them.

Father Joe's crucifix and the relics given to Humphrey's mother from Father Joe

During his years in South Boston Father Joe devoted most of his free time to the youth. I asked Norma and Humphrey what they thought drove him to spend so much of his time with its youth and youth gangs. Norma said it was his personality; he could always talk with people and influence both young and old. Humphrey said that he had a charisma as a leader, not a follower. He went on to say that the kind of respect he saw from the young people in South Boston was that same respect from young people in Haverhill. Both Norma and Humphrey felt that there was something inside Father Joe that pushed him to help troubled youth and conduct religious activities for them.

Norma first learned of Joe's diagnosis of leukemia from his mother, she couldn't believe it because he looked so healthy. Norma remembers the day Father Joe told her he was being transferred from St. Monica's to Gate of Heaven in South Boston. He told Norma that he was told the transfer was because of his illness. He said that the Cardinal and others did not feel he could continue to perform his priestly duties. He was upset with his transfer and didn't want to leave St. Monica's. The Cardinal allowed him to stay in South Boston and transferred him to Gate of Heaven Parish, only 1.5 miles away.

Norma remembered that Cardinal Cushing visited Joe when he was very ill. The Cardinal told him not to worry about his mother, that he would take care of her. After Father Joe's death, with the help of Cardinal Cushing, his mother went to live at a Catholic assisted-living facility called, D'Youville in Lowell, MA.

Humphrey describes how it had been a true honor in his life to be one of the pallbearers at Father Joe's funeral. He will never forget the hundreds of people, young and old who attended the services and the five-mile-long motorcade back to Haverhill to bury him in St. James Cemetery. "It was such a fitting tribute to a man who gave so much of himself to the priesthood and the people of South Boston," said Humphrey.

Norma, looking back, always had a special place in her heart for Joe. She still has a Saint Teresa relic that belonged to Father Joe and will always treasure it. She stated, "He took his vocation seriously and wanted to be the best servant of God he could be. In his almost six years as a priest, he left a legacy that we honor to this day. We will never forget the impact that he had on the lives of his family members and the many that he served as a priest."

AUTHOR'S MEMORIES

GROWING UP IN THE OLD HABOR VILLAGE PROJECT

I grew up in the 1950s and 1960s in South Boston, Massachusetts which is a section of Boston, affectionately referred to as "Southie." South Boston covers 3.72 square miles, and was predominately white Irish, blue-collar, working-poor at that time. It was the home to the likes of Archbishop of Boston Richard Cardinal Cushing, John W. McCormack, Speaker of the House of Representatives, Senator William Bulger, President of the Massachusetts Senate, Congressman Joseph Moakley and Representative Michael F. Flaherty and Raymond Flynn, Mayor of Boston. My world revolved around the streets of the Old Harbor Village Housing Project, the first public housing development in the United States. It was comprised of more than 1000 apartments, 22 three-story buildings and 752 row houses. Everyone knew each other, parents knew other parents, they watched their own children and their neighbors' children, as well as their dogs and cats who roamed freely around the projects. It was not uncommon for neighbors to knock on each other's door for milk, eggs or sugar, or perhaps to babysit for an hour. It was a simple life back then. There was no air conditioning in the project apartments so during the warmer months all our windows remained opened. However, we never feared being robbed because our neighbors were our neighborhood's eyes and ears. We had Mrs. Mettrick on the first floor, Mrs. Sullivan on the second floor and Mrs. Henderson on the third floor.

Father Joe

During the summer evenings we would often see them hanging out their windows seeking relief from their blazing hot apartments. They were mostly stay-at-home moms whose husbands went out to a blue-collar job daily. My Mom, however, was a single Mom who had to work to support us. She was lucky enough to get a job at the local drug store, often called 'the druggie' which was across the street from our projects. It was more than a drug store; it was the local candy store with a counter and swivel stools for ice cream cones, frappes, or a tonic. The fact that my mom worked there was good and bad for me. Everyone knew her and would report on my shenanigans every time they visited the 'druggie'. Life in the projects was full of amusing sights and sounds! I remember during summer you would see, hear, and smell the 'Rag Man', riding his horse-drawn wagon up and down the project streets. He was a large man, with a long white bushy beard wearing what looked like a red and blue circus coat, a large straw cowboy hat. He accepted rags or old clothes brought to him. His trademark advertising was yelling, "Rags, Rags, Rags," until some resident ran out and handed him some old clothes for maybe ten cents a pound. He would stop to accept the goods from the project residents and his smelly horse would think it a good time to relieve himself in the middle of the street, added to the already bad stench from a nearby dump. In the hot summer months, we could not only smell the horse but could also smell and see the trail of horse dump left behind. Living in the projects we did not have much grass, mostly concrete and not all owners cleaned up after their dogs. Many just left it on the ground for the rainy days to wash it away. You can imagine the smells permeating from the nearby dump added to that what was left behind from the horses and the dogs! It's a smell I can still remember to this day.

Most families lived in the three-story brick buildings and each building had its own, "incinerator," a garbage disposal system. A week did not go by without the Boston Fire Department having to respond to one or more of the buildings. Fires would break out because many residents or kids would dump not just garbage, but everything but the kitchen sink down the chute. It was always exciting to see the brave Boston firemen responding in our time of need and it provided a source of 'entertainment' for all the kids in the project, but not for the firemen, who had to deal with the incinerator fires and the dangerous toxic fumes. These types of fires prompted the fireman to pack dozens of bricks on the fire trucks to throw down the incinerators to help put out the fires. Then there was election-season fiasco which was always predictable about 1 to 2 weeks before an election. Two maybe three days a week several vehicles with a giant speaker on the roofs of their cars would ride up and down the project streets playing John Phillip Sousa music to remind the residents to vote for their candidate on election day. The bullhorn on wheels was so loud and annoying, especially while I was trying to watch *"The Three Stooges"* or *"Gunsmoke"* and there was always a chance you would miss the whole show because of the noise.

Sports have always been a big deal in Boston, starting early in life with the youth. The projects had 3 or 4 basketball courts that were used day and night with an unwritten rule that after a certain time during the weeknights the games would stop. However, on the weekends the field lights would remain on later and playing would go on late into the night. Hockey in the winter was played on the snow and ice-covered streets. In the summer the baseball fields were easily accessible since they were directly across from the projects on Morrissey Boulevard. Winters meant plenty of snow and after a Boston blizzard, parking in the projects was at a premium. Residents would spend hours shoveling their cars out before work and then 'save their spot' with a trash can, a box or even a statue of the Blessed Mother. Beware the repercussions to anyone who would dare move that object and park in 'their' spot!

South Boston was saturated with youth gangs and many kids joined a gang to survive life on the streets. You had your choice of gangs such as, The Mullins, Redwings, Blackhawks, Saints, Rebels, Cavaliers, Killeens, Shamrocks, Gustins and many others. Some were more rebellious than others. Gangs were active planning fights, thefts, and other mischief. On Sundays, there was a cease-fire for the day. Everyone was expected to show up for Mass. You had your choice of times and could choose either the upstairs church or the downstairs church; Masses went on all morning. I became part of one of these gang which led to my relationship with the parish priest. This is where I met and began my relationship with Father Joseph E. Laporte.

There is so much more that could be written about growing up in South Boston and life in the projects. However, this story is not about living in the projects, and not about me, but about a Roman Catholic priest and why a statue of him and a young boy stands today on Columbia Road in South Boston. Joseph E. Laporte was that priest and through this story we hope to preserve the legacy of a priest who had a profound effect upon everyone he met.

St. Monica's Parish was directly across the street from the Old Harbor Village projects. With the support of St. Monica's pastor, Father Joe took the Cardinal's words to heart "look after its youth" and began making contact with the project's youth. One of his aims was to try and move as many young men as possible away from gang influences toward other interests. However, aside from confronting the gang members he would also have interactions with their parents, the police, lawyers, judges, elected officials, merchants, teachers, and some unhappy church parishioners. When he was not carrying out his official priestly duties such as celebrating Mass, administering the sacraments, visiting the sick in the hospital or in their homes, he organized the Young Adult Missions each year, oversaw bingo and other fundraisers, recruited and trained altar boys, the choir and fulfilled many other duties. His free time was spent with the young men and boys of the parish getting to know them better. Father Laporte learned that many of them came from good families and were raised by both parents or by one parent, mostly by their mothers, such as me. He used to think that these gang members came from single parent homes, but learned they came from both types of homes, even the most loving homes. I will never know what drove him to try and help the Southie boys, but it

Father Joe

seemed to be what consumed his daily work and very being. There were some St. Monica's parishioners who strongly disagreed with his connection with the boys. They complained to him after Mass, and to his pastor. Word got around the parish that these same parishioners even sent letters to the Cardinal criticizing Father Laporte. They complained about him taking off his cassock, especially his clerical white collar, and playing basketball in the projects with us. They called his conduct sacrilegious! They complained about Father Laporte hearing confession outside the church confessional: they pointed to his habit of hearing confessions of the youth in his car. Father Joe was different than other priests we knew. On scorching summer nights, he would take off his white collar, four-pointed biretta and black cassock, and play basketball with us. He walked around the projects and interacted with our parents and neighbors. He would make it a point to try and speak to the families of kids he was trying to help. During these conversations he would tell the parents about the many church activities in which he could use the help and talents of their sons or daughters. Father Laporte, a good judge of character, was not afraid to recruit gang members as altar boys, choir singers, or Confraternity of Christian Doctrine (CCD) instructors---he talked me into all three! Becoming involved in the church that way could get you labeled a sissy. He took a lot of criticism for this practice, but this was his way of building a bridge between the youth and the church. It got me off the streets and could have been the turning point in my life from a life of crime to a life of duty and achievement. I took the latter and I owe that to Father Joe. During my service

28

as an altar boy, I recall when I reported at 6:30 a.m. for the 7 a.m. Mass I would always see Father Joe kneeling in front of the Blessed Mother altar. He was there before the church lights were fully turned on and looked deep in prayer.

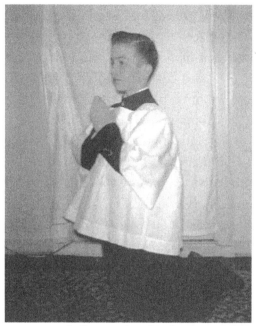

Author as an altar boy

Going to church for confession on Saturday evening, the wait was always longer for Father Laporte's confessional. Both young and old waited their turn to confess to him. When he heard a familiar voice, he was known for saying, "Oh, you again'" or "I missed you at last Sunday's Mass". Father Laporte's demeanor, and his compassionate attitude when listening to disturbing behavior always seemed to make you

Father Joe

feel that it was never too late to turn things around. He had a way with words, making you see the harm you were doing to yourself. He reminded you of the person you were stealing from and how they were suffering. He would remind you of the hurt you were causing your mother or father and the harm to their reputations. We would see him in our schools, at the police station and local court room. He would never condone the trouble we got ourselves into, but just his presence let us know of his care and concern. He would show up on street corners where we hung out at night. He wouldn't spend a lot of time, but just long enough to say hello to everyone, offer confession, or just talk about the Red Sox, Patriots, Celtics, or the Bruins. For many of the project residents, seeing and speaking with Father Laporte was highly valued. His presence and a personal interest in their children were something they couldn't get enough of. It was seen as genuine and greatly appreciated by the parents, especially those who were finding it difficult and needed the help raising these youngsters.

What made Father Laporte stand out from other priests was his approach; he treated everyone with respect, never talking down to you. He spoke to you as if he was a big brother and you always felt his true concern for his interest in your schoolwork or your free-time activities. He was not intimidating even though he stood more than 6 feet tall with dark hair, dark eyes, a lean and athletic build, always wearing his long black cassock and his four-point biretta (except when he took it off to play ball with us). He drove a beat-up 4-door sedan, a car you would hear before you saw it coming. When he drove away it look like a smoke screen for Navy ships.

Southie Will Never Forget You

Thinking back, many of us wanted to get him a new car, but we knew he would never accept anything stolen.

Father Joe was like the big brother or the father we never had. He had a great sense of humor, on the basketball court, in church, or even when hearing your confession. For instance, he could find something in your playing, then annoy you about it which provoked you to play better. Another funny example of his sense of humor was one Ash Wednesday when we decided not to go to church to get ashes on our foreheads. We instead found some coal and placed a cross on each other's foreheads. That afternoon Father Joe drove to where we were hanging out. He pulled up, rolled his window down and was looking at our foreheads. He smiled and said, "looks good, boys." He looked down at my dirty hands, shaking his head and saying, "You forgot to wash your hands." He laughed and drove away!

The drug store on Devine Way, called "the druggie", was a popular hangout for us. It was one of many stops where Father Joe would hear confessions in his car. On Saturday nights he would drive up to the druggie and ask if anyone wanted to receive the Sacrament of Penance. He would tell us that he would be parked in the field, which was across the street. He would also leave the back door to his vehicle unlocked and never look to see who was coming into the 'confessional'. No one cared who went and you always felt better after receiving his absolution and blessing.

Although all of us respected Father Laporte, we were not always honest with him. Looking back, we were only hurting ourselves, but as teens we thought we were smarter than he was. How naive we were to think that! Father Joe spent so much of his time interacting with us. Besides playing basketball, baseball, and handball, organizing church activities and bus trips, he broke up fights and defused impending fights among rival gangs. Father Joe never took sides, he looked for peaceful ways out of conflicts. While there were many gang members he could not turn around, it never stopped him from trying. When in their company he would always address them with respect by saying, "Hello, how are you". To the ones who did not attend Mass, he would always say, "See you at Sunday Mass." But even among the few that did not go to church and were very vocal about not needing religion, they also respected him. As a priest, Father Joe was like no other priest I knew. As an altar boy, I watched him interact with young and old alike, and admired how he treated everyone with respect and kindness. However, I also noticed he would never hesitate to admonish bad behavior from anyone. Father Joe never lost his common touch with the people; it didn't matter who he was standing with, he would acknowledge you with just his look and a smile. After Mass he would always remain at the front door of the church speaking to parishioners until they all left.

My first real sense of loss in my life came in May 1963 when Father Joe was transferred from Saint Monica's Parish to Gate of Heaven Parish just 1.5 miles away. I can still remember the very lonely feeling I experienced when I reported for altar boy service the first time after he left for his new assignment. I opened the door to the church and did not see Father Joe kneeling at the Blessed Mother altar. I felt an overwhelming sadness and emptiness. I lost not just my priest but a best friend. I vividly recall the empty feeling I felt that day because I looked up to him as the big brother I never had. What made the situation more painful was that I had overheard him telling a fellow priest he did not want to leave Saint Monica's. He was my confidant and my trusted friend. For many years I shared my inner-most secrets, that not even my mother knew, with him in confession. He had counseled me for many months, gently guiding me to reform my ways, advising me how I could be a better person and to always pray to Mary and Jesus. Frankly, I was mad at God for taking him from St. Monica's and away from me. Life without the person you love hurts and for a while, you feel alone. However, I soon got over my anger because Father Joe (true to form) never forgot us. We soon began to see him again walking around the Old Harbor project, playing basketball and hearing confessions. It was a wonderful feeling!

Then the news came that he was diagnosed with leukemia; I was shocked, devastated, and did not want to believe it. He was suffering with the symptoms of leukemia for a long time before his diagnosis but never, never showed any obvious signs of being sick. Many of my friends and I never really understood how seriously ill he was; he never talked about his illness or complained of being sick. But that was the kind of man he was, unselfish. He thought only of our welfare.

When he told the Cardinal of his diagnosis, the Cardinal

thought a transfer to a more suitable assignment would be in his best interest. It is reported that Father Joe responded, "Please leave me in South Boston, I would rather wear away than rust away doing nothing."

It was my freshman year at South Boston High School when the untimely death of Father Laporte happened on March 13, 1965. During my high school years, I could still hear his voice and feel his presence. There were numerous incidents within this time when I could still hear him in my head telling me to consider the consequences before I made a bad choice. He would say, "Think of the hurt and shame you will bring upon your mother." His example had a profound influence on me, so much so that I was seriously considering entering the priesthood. At the time, I wanted to do the same type of work Father Laporte was doing working with the youth. However, what stopped me from entering the priesthood was having no brothers or sisters. I knew my mother would never have any grandchildren. This was during the time of the Vietnam War when I and many of my friends were faced with the draft. If I needed to serve, I wanted a choice. Therefore, shortly after graduation at 18 years old, I enlisted in the United States Marine Corps. Following boot camp at Marine Corp Base Parris Island and some specialized training with the United States Army, I was deployed to Da Nang, Vietnam with the 1st Marine Division.

Sgt. Stafford, USMC

Before my discharge from USMC, I was assigned to the 4th Marine Division, Marine Corps Reserve, Boston, Massachusetts until 1974. I decided that I didn't want to return to South Boston because I knew deep in my heart that I would go back to hanging out on the corner and being exposed to bad influences. It was at this point I realized that I wanted more for my life. Long story short, I became a police officer in New Brunswick, New Jersey which led to my tenure at Middlesex County Prosecutor's Office, New Jersey Division of Criminal Justice, Office of Government Integrity and New Jersey Office of Homeland Security and Preparedness. Shortly after I arrived in New Jersey, I met and married my wife, Emma; we have four daughters.

Although it has been almost 60 years since his death, I will never forget Father Joe and all that he did for me in my formative years. I will honor him always for he was truly a saint in my life who I had the privilege to walk beside.

"Do not forget those who have had charge of you, and preached God's word to you: contemplate the happy issue of the life they lived and imitate their faith." Heb, 13:7

Inscription on the base of the Father Laporte statue.

CLOSE FRIENDS OF FATHER JOE

Bob Derrah

Left to right: Jack Hurley, Bob Derrah, Billy Shed, Kenny Paulsen

I lived in the Old Harbor Village on 14 Logan Way, South Boston attended South Boston High School and graduated with the class of 1958. I can still remember the day the newly ordained priest, Father Joseph Laporte, arrived at St. Monica's Parish in 1959. He stood over 6-foot tall with jet black hair, which matched his long black cassock and the four-pointed biretta that he wore on his head. Between that first day in 1959 until his untimely death on March 13,1965, I had many encounters and became very close with Father Joe, as we affectionately called him. What I most remember was Father Joe doing things that I had never seen any other priest do. I spent my summers as a lifeguard at Carson Beach, the local beach for the residents of Old Harbor Village. It was common to see Father Joe taking a swim and then talking and interacting with many of the beachgoers. Another uncommon thing was to see a priest in the 1950s roll up his sleeves and play a game of basketball with the kids who lived in the projects. There were several basketball courts within Old Harbor Village and Father Joe made it a practice to frequent them often. No other priest ever paid that much attention to Southie's youth.

Another vivid memory of him was how he would hear our confessions. The sacrament of Penance, as far as I knew, was always held in the 'lower' Church, usually on Saturday afternoon. The expectation was that all who were going to receive Communion on Sunday would go to church Saturday to confess their sins to the priest. When we didn't show up for confession on Saturday afternoon, Father Joe would come find us Saturday night at the street corner, at the beach, or wherever we were and hear our confessions on the spot. Father Joe would drive up to a street, see a group of youth, pull up and offer to hear their confessions in his car. He would be in the front seat; we would get in the rear seat. The oddest thing, though, was receiving the sacrament of Penance at the beach.

I recall being invited to Father Joe's hometown Haverhill, MA and meeting his mother and father; they were warm and welcoming and invited us to eat with them.

For the short time he was assigned to St. Monica's, he had become very close with its youth and did more for them than any previous priest. I remember in 1963 Father Joe was suddenly transferred to Gate of Heaven Parish, another Catholic Church in the same town. I felt a sense of loss and many of the residents were disappointed that he had been taken away from us. In the subsequent months, the community learned of his illness, that he was extremely sick and were saddened to hear he was diagnosed with leukemia.

Approximately 6 months before his death, a committee was formed in South Boston and a huge Tribute Dinner was held in honor of Father Joe at Blinstrub's, the legendary nightclub in Southie at corner of D Street and West Broadway. It was a sold-out event attended by his fellow priests, nuns, civic leaders, and many of Southie's young people.

On March 13,1965 news of Father Joe's death spread like wildfire in South Boston. To me and many of our close friends his death was not unexpected because we knew his prognosis was not good. It was a sad day for all of us. But there was a strange occurrence that took place on the evening of Fr. Joe's death. My friend, Ken Paulsen, told me that he called the hospital to talk to Fr. Joe. Normally, the call would go through the switchboard, but strangely, Fr. Joe answered the telephone and they had a conversation. Later, Ken was told that Fr. Joe had died three hours before their conversation! How is this possible? Is this a miracle?

Father Joe

John Simpson

Left to right: Sal Cardella, Frannie Madden, Bob Ciulla, John Simpson

My Dad passed away when I was four years old, whereupon my mother moved to the Old Harbor Projects; I was raised at 261 O'Callaghan Way, South Boston. I recall my first contact with Father Laporte was in the Fall of 1960. My friends and I were playing basketball at the courts in the projects. I recognized him as the new priest at Saint Monica's Parish who everyone in the projects was talking about. He would come often to play basketball with us. He was a bull and fooled around a lot while playing. One time, while we were playing, my mother invited Father Joe to join our family for a simple baked macaroni dinner and he, surprisedly, accepted. We found out it was a favorite dinner of his and subsequently, we invited him any time my mother was making baked macaroni. I remember hearing through the projects complaints some residents were raising with Saint Monica's pastor. Apparently, Father Joe was sent to Saint Monica's parish to work with its youth. Some project residents did not approve of Father Laporte's interaction with us, such as playing basketball, and they would report their dismay to the rectory. During one dinner with our family, he did divulge having been reprimanded by the monsignor for the methods he was using to reach the South Boston youth.

Father Laporte had a way about him so that you knew he was sincere. You knew you could trust him. You could talk to him about anything, and I believe I did. Often, we would be walking down the street, could be anywhere in Southie, when Father Joe would pull up to us in his car. He would ask if any of us had been to confession recently, if not, he would hear our confessions in his car, right then and there.

One Saturday, Millie Hutchinson (now my wife), and I went to Saint Monica's to receive the Sacrament of Penance. We ended up on opposite sides of the confessional at the same time with Father Laporte in its center. He suddenly opened both sliding windows and asked us how we were both doing. Millie was mortified. Then he said, "I hope there's been none of that cheap physical stuff going on with you two." We bowed our heads and said the Act of Contrition. Millie still talks about that story to this day. Another memory of the respect that Southie youth had for him was at Saint Monica's weeklong, "Young Adult Mission."

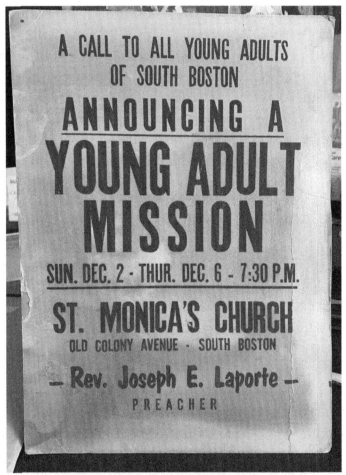

Flyer for Young Adult Mission held by Father Joe

Father Joe planned, organized, and ran these weeklong Young Adult Missions, and took great pride in its purpose of helping Southie's youth.

Southie Will Never Forget You

During the Mission, I recall how Father Laporte would tell us every night that he was hoping Cardinal Cushing would be celebrating Mass on the last day. I remember how upset he was that he had not been able to connect with the Cardinal. Finally, a night before the last day he got to meet with the Cardinal. He told the Cardinal how the church had been filled every night of the Mission with young people. He also told the Cardinal what an honor it would be if he would celebrate the closing Mass. I recall hearing rumors through the grape vine that the Cardinal was very skeptical of a church full of South Boston teenagers. No way! After some time, Father Joe, as only he could, convinced the Cardinal to celebrate Mass at Saint Monica's on the Mission's last day. As Cardinal Cushing in all his splendor drove up to Saint Monica's for that closing Mass, he could not believe his eyes. He saw all the youth standing in front of the entrance doors of the church, down both sides of the stairs and on both sides of the sidewalk. When Cardinal Cushing spoke at the Mass, he praised the youth of South Boston. When addressing the standing room only church he told the youth, he "knew all along that there would be a great turnout for this last Mass of the Young Adult Mission". Of course, he did! After all the Cardinal was born and raised in Southie himself!

One night after a game of basketball at Southie High, Father Laporte drove me home. I could see he was in a lot of pain and my heart sank! That night Frannie Madden (my friend and best man) and I went to Saint Monica's Rectory to see Father Laporte. He told us he had been diagnosed with leukemia and asked us not to say anything.

Father Joe

After my graduation from South Boston High School in 1962 I enlisted in the United States Navy and was serving on the USS Pocono. While I was home on military leave Father Laporte was taken to the hospital. Fran Madden, my girlfriend Millie, and I attempted to visit him at the New England Baptist Hospital on the night before he passed away. We were unable to see him because he was in such terrible pain. The next day I had to return to my ship in Norfolk, Virginia whereupon Millie telephoned to tell me that Father Laporte had died. I was unable to attend any of his funeral services, but Millie had attended and wrote me about the turn out. As for Millie and I, we lost our best friend that night; it was a very emotional time. Father Joe had blessed her engagement ring and had promised to marry us. That was not to be; he died before he could keep that promise. Subsequently, we were married on May 21,1966 at Saint Monica's Parish. Both Millie and I could not help thinking of Father LaPorte, and there was no question that we both felt his presence.

I believe it was for our 5th wedding anniversary, when Frannie Madden commissioned an artist neighbor of his to paint a portrait of Father Laporte from a photo. The woman who painted this portrait did a lot of research on Father Laporte. She became so impressed with his story she wanted to keep it for herself. She did give it up and it has hung in our home over 50 years.

John Simpson and his son with Father Laporte portrait.

Being brought up Catholic and looking back at that time
in my life, I was led to believe that priests were to be put on a
pedestal. Father Joe showed all of us that priests were human
beings just like the rest of us. There was never an air about
him, and he had a calling to do God's work. He did it his way,
maybe not to the liking of a few, but he did more during his
short time on earth, especially for the youth of South Boston,
than most priests could have done in 30 or even 40 years of

Father Joe

service to God. Father Laporte's honesty, (to a fault at times), integrity and trustworthiness were without a doubt the reason the youth flocked to him the way they did. Father Joe treated us with respect, and when he noticed someone not behaving, he would tell them to their face. Lastly, it is tough to say what Father Joe's legacy would be. I believe WE are his legacy, all of us whose lives he touched while serving God on Earth, right here in South Boston.

Frannie Madden

Frannie and his daughter, Michelle Laporte Madden Brent

I first met Father Joe in 1960 through my friend, John Simpson, who lived in the Old Harbor Village Projects, South Boston. I lived at 103 H. Street, in Southie, known as City Point, but I hung out at Old Harbor. I was a Gate of Heaven parishioner and attended South Boston High School and graduated in 1963.

I would see Father Joe at least once a week, (sometimes more), while he played basketball with my gang, the 2nd St. Gang, on Wednesday nights at South Boston High School. John Simpson and I would stop by Saint Monica's rectory when Father Joe had the duty, which he was not crazy about. One priest had to be at the rectory per order of the pastor.

Father Joe

Father Joe wanted to be out with the kids.

Sometimes we would head over to Ho Jo's, (Howard Johnson restaurant), for a black and white frappe, Father Joe's favorite. I recall seeing him quite frequently for confession or just to hang out with John and my friends. If he didn't see you at confession, he went looking for you. He knew where every kid in Southie, "hung out." Father Joe was, "on patrol" all over Southie, day and night.

I was a member of the Gate of Heaven Parish, but due to my friendship with John, I spent more time at Saint Monica's. One memory I have was being invited by Father Joe with another friend to his boyhood home in Haverhill, Massachusetts. On the car ride to Haverhill, Father Joe filled us with horror stories of his mom. He told us that his mom drank a lot of wine and may be laying on the floor when we got there. We met Father Joe's mom and aunt and were invited for dinner. His mom was a sweet lady and a great cook. They were both very cordial to us and made us feel at home. Of course, that talk about his mom was Father Joe just being a comedian. He really had a Southie sense of humor!

Father Joe could make a teaching experience out of just about anything. In the 1960s there was a Rock 'n Roll song by Gene McDaniels, "Chip Chip." The lyrics went something like: "chip, chip, you tell a little lie…, chip, chip, you cheat a little bit…, One day you are gonna discover, one little wrong leads to another…chip, chip, chippin' away". His interpretation was spot on; first you start lying about the little things and before you know it, you destroy something beautiful. That was a life lesson and I have never forgotten it.

Southie Will Never Forget You

I remember how Father Joe would give you, 'the look,' if you said something he did not like. Like the time I yelled across the street to him, "Hey, Joe," just to see what would happen. I got, 'the look'. It could knock you down. When shaking your hand, he had a vice grip that could cause you to lose feeling in your hand. He no longer had that power when he got sick. That's when I knew the rumors of his illness were true.

Father Joe was transferred to Gate of Heaven Parish in 1963 in hopes that he would cut back on his activities and rest more. It was just the opposite. He started an organization for young people and threw himself into it. He worked harder than ever. He also organized and ran "The Young Adult Missions," and was able to enlist the Archbishop of Boston, Cardinal Cushing to say the Mass on the last day of the Mission. These were a huge success.

I remember one late evening, as Father Joe and I were walking down the street in Southie we observed a poor guy sitting on the curb with his head down looking at the gutter. As we walked past him Father Joe stopped and pressed some money into his hand. I recall him saying to me, "Fella' might be hungry, you know Fran."

Father Joe was a young man when he arrived at Saint Monica's Parish. He routinely joined in games with us in the projects, we had never experienced a priest doing this before. His message to us was do the right thing, never ruin anyone's reputation, never talk about anyone badly. If you slammed anyone he would always say, "That's funny he speaks well of you."

Father Joe

I remember Father Joe driving up to street corners where we hung out and hearing our confessions on these street corners or in his car. We thought his hearing confession in his car was the coolest thing ever. If he didn't see you, he went looking for you.

On many occasions Father Joe would appear at South Boston's Municipal District Court. He would be there to vouch for some kid that had gotten into trouble. He would pay a visit to the principal of South Boston High School and ask that the kid be reinstated after being suspended.

For me, I just wanted to be a better person and never disappoint him. Father Joe touched so many lives it was just a natural thing to have a statue to honor him. People loved Father Joe and his great sense of humor. When asked where he was from, he always answered "Southie." As I have said many times, Father Joe was a wonderful priest, and a great guy but more than anything he was my friend. My wife and I decided to give our daughter Michelle the middle name 'Laporte' as a lasting tribute.

Joe Sheppeck

Left to right: Bob Derrah, Joe Sheppeck, Michael Stedman

Two thoughts come to mind when I hear the name Father Laporte, or Father Joe, as we liked to call him. I remember him as a parish priest during the late 1950's and early 1960's who was an admired friend of South Boston's youth and someone who loved the town of South Boston.

The Sheppeck's, six children and our parents, lived in a five-room apartment, (three bedrooms), at 417 Old Colony Ave, Old Harbor Village. After being schooled locally until ninth grade I attended Boston Technical High School for one and a half years. I then transferred to South Boston and graduated in 1958. Upon graduation I enlisted in the United

Father Joe

States Army reserves and then attended Boston State College for four years, graduating in 1964.

My parents, two brothers, three sisters and myself participated in Saint Monica's parish activities. When my mother died in 1957 the younger siblings had the support from the priests in the church, since they saw us on a daily basis. The older children attended the 7:00 a.m. Mass at Saint Monica's before work in memory of our mother. My involvement with Father Laporte was as a member of a group of eight close friends; Father Joe became a mentor, an advisor and a buddy to us all. As our lives became more focused the bonds varied from frequent contact to periods of inactivity. But he was always there for most of us. Remember, we were only one small group of several young people that he had in his circle. There were several other priests who were also assigned to Saint Monica's Parish. They were the pastor, Monsignor Golden, Father McGrath and Father McGlone who were all very close to my sisters. However, it was Father Laporte who was more accessible to my brothers and myself. And that was key! I found that Father Laporte repeated this trait with many others. He always seemed to be available. Word spread that the new priest, Father Joe, was reaching out to the young crowd. I was a member of a crew of eight to ten guys, not a gang, just a tight group who shared the same interests. Playing baseball, part-time work, hanging out, self-protection, etc. Some to a greater degree than others. No matter the degree, all were respectful of Father Laporte. My brothers, John and Gerard, shared the same opinions of Father Laporte. I recall John, a year younger than I, who was eager to learn how to drive a car. John's eagerness to learn and to get more practice behind the wheel reached Saint Monica's Rectory whereupon Father Laporte offered to teach him using his own car. An unusual gift for a priest to give a youngster however, it is a typical example of his generous and caring nature.

Another memory of the respect and influence that the youth in Southie had for Father Laporte was their attendance at St. Monica's weeklong Young Adult Missions. Father Joe organized and ran these missions and took great pride in its aim to speak to teens about the problems of young adults and to have some fun, planned activities. It was always a success.

One of our crew, Alan Mac, became particularly close to Fr. Joe. Alan was a college candidate, more of a go-getter than the rest of us. He became a good buddy of Father Joe. Alan went off to Boston University, whereas five other crew members enlisted in the United States Army Military Reserves in 1959. During our time in the military, we kept in touch with one another by US mail. During this same period, we learned that Alan Mac had become seriously ill with leukemia. We all felt so helpless not being there to help and support Alan. However, Father Laporte WAS there for him, a very fortunate, yet characteristic response. They were both dealing with life and death issues at the time, unbeknownst to us. It was divine intervention, I guess, and his prayers and support for Alan and his family helped them during this very emotional period. When I returned to Southie in 1960, I learned that there was no cure. Alan had no hope for recovery. Our crew all bonded together again but by the end of 1960 Alan passed away and

Father Joe

Father Laporte had presided over his funeral.

Father Laporte had remarkable abilities to engage the parish youth with his use of social worker skills and a common sense in dealing with issues that confront projects' kids. It was always amazing to me that Father Laporte, who was raised in suburban Haverhill, MA, had such a common touch with city youth. Here was a man who came from a somewhat sheltered background, lacking any exposure to poor urban issues and the associated baggage and yet he was able to assimilate himself so gracefully into the lives of so many of us. I wonder if this was a cause of conflict in the rectory, for example, he was working so hard and long with the young vs. spending more time with the more conservative church groups. Father Laporte's nontraditional approach brought more kids into the parish activities. His priestly activities in dealing with many teenagers in the projects caused some gossip. I was aware of some push-back by some members of Saint Monica's Parish who did not approve of his outreach methods and friendships with the youth. This push-back also came from the pastor and some colleagues at Saint Monica's. The Cardinal must have been aware of his activities and friendships with many of the young people of both Old Harbor Village and Old Colony Projects. These methods by Father Laporte may have been the underlining reason for his transfer.

Soon after the death of Alan Mac, I met my future wife, Claire Gilligan from Roslindale at Boston State College. I had the pleasure to introduce Claire to Father Laporte and we talked of our plans to marry. He sensed that we were serious, but too young, (22 and 20 years old), for the Sacrament of Matrimony. He was aware of the risks involved. Father Laporte told us to bide our time.

A new chapter began for Father Joe when he was transferred to Gate of Heaven Parish in Southie. A sad day at Saint Monica's but more important he remained in town and extended his influence on a new group of youth. I got very busy at school and was working long hours at work and lost touch, until I heard of his illness. I lost the close connection we had in the early years, but I was kept informed of the prognosis. It was very sad personally because I had lost my friend, Alan, so recently and now the same diagnosis for Father Joe, another special friend in my life. After Father Laporte's death, life went on -- marriage, kids, careers. He was always in our thoughts, and I always wished he could have presided at our wedding, baptized our boys and celebrated our 50th wedding anniversary with us. We know he was there in spirit!

John O'Connor

1967 Teacher of Business, Dorchester High School

My name is John O'Connor (Okie) Jr, born and raised in South Boston, City Point area, across the street from M Street Beach on Marine Road and a short walk to L Street Bath House. I graduated from Boston English High School in 1953 and Providence College in 1962. I received my Master's degree from Boston College in Economics.

Father Laporte was assigned to Saint Monica's in 1959 and after he was diagnosed with leukemia he was transferred to Gate of Heaven Parish by Richard Cardinal Cushing. I first met Father Joe in 1962 at the L Street Bath House, where he developed an extraordinary relationship with the youth of South Boston. He would hear confessions on the beach or in his car, on a regular basis. Many of our group would have our confessions heard at Saint Monica's on Saturday nights. During one of those confessions, I tried to disguise my deep voice in the confessional. Afterwards as I was walking down the aisle Fr. Joe shouted loud enough for all to hear; "Great confession John," with his great sense of humor and laugh. I enjoyed playing basketball with Father Joe in the municipal building on Broadway. When my father died in 1963 Father Joe was a great source of friendship, advice, and comfort. I have never known a priest like Father Joe. When my son John III was dying at the age of 45 in 2012, he remarked that God must be mad at him. I told him that the saintliest man I had ever known, Father Joe, died at the age of 32 from the same diagnosis. I assured him God was not mad at him.

Sometime after Father Joe was transferred to Gate of Heaven Parish, he asked many of the recent college graduates, including myself, if we would be interested in forming a youth club called, "CHI-RIO," for Southie youth between the ages of 18 and 25. I accepted. Most of the committee were fellow lifeguards and within a short period it was an instant success. Father Joe spoke about problems of young adults and activities were planned. Everything we did was well attended as result of the love and inspiration shown by Father Joe. Whoever heard of Southie kids attending Old Timers Night at the Boston Pops. We sold it out. However, the most outstanding trip was a three-day bus trip to an Inn in the North Conway, New Hampshire. After a great time skiing and partying we were on our way home when our bus broke down in Milton, New Hampshire. We were fortunate to be able to

Father Joe

stay at a church hall during the night, while awaiting the new buses. However only one bus arrived, and it was decided to take the young ladies home first. While we (the boys) waited for the second bus, Father Joe decided to celebrate Mass in the hall at 3:00 a.m.---everyone attended. Just another example of how Father Laporte influenced all of us. In 1963 we were informed that Father Joe had been diagnosed with leukemia, but he never talked about it nor did it slow him down, until several months before he died.

Because of the tremendous love for Father Joe, we decided to form a committee to organize a Night of Appreciation at Blinstrubs Night Club. John Connolly, Jr was Chairman; Jack Dever, Secretary; Warren Toland, Treasurer; Publicity, Ray Flynn and Bob Monahan. Many other close friends were on the committee. The night of the celebration was sold out and many folks were disappointed that they were unable to attend. Those of us who were lucky enough to attend this tribute knew how much it meant to Father Joe.

I was fortunate to visit him in the hospital before he passed on March 13,1965. With direction and assistance from Father White, arrangements were made for the funeral at Gate of Heaven Church.

I, along with John Connolly Jr, Jimbo Daly, Tom Kelley, Pat Munroe and Bob O'Brien were honored to be selected as pallbearers. The church was filled to capacity while hundreds stood outside to demonstrate their love for Father Joe. Those of us who were close to Father Joe were so saddened that we decided to meet and come up with a way to memorialize him. I was selected as Chairman and Jack Dever was made

Southie Will Never Forget You

Treasurer. After several meetings we decided that a statue honoring Father Joe with a young boy at his side would be right. For many Friday nights, because that was 'pay day', we went door to door asking South Boston residents for any amount of money to build Father Joe's statue. We used paper bags to collect any amount of coins and bills. We were able to have South Boston's weekly newspaper, the South Boston Tribune, print the names and amount of their contributions on its front page. My best recollection is that not one person refused to donate. After we finished all the numbered and letter streets in town, we decided to try the numerous pubs in South Boston. Father Laporte touched all South Boston youth, even gang members. Jack Dever and I went to a bar on West Broadway and when we entered, we noticed a table of several Mullin Gang members. Although I tried to avoid them, they wanted to know what I was doing. I told them we were collecting funds for a Father Laporte statue. One of the gang members gave me a handful of cash totaling $200! After several weeks we were able to raise $10,000 in cash just using paper bags. It took several years for the statue to become a reality, but we never gave up. The committee awarded the building of the statue to Daprato Company of Charlestown. It was decided that the statue would be of Father Laporte and a young boy standing atop an Italian marble pedestal. Father Paul White, who later became editor of the Pilot Catholic Newspaper, provided much assistance to the committee and selected the inscription on the statue.

Statue unveiling at the dedication, April 21, 1968

We hoped to place the statue on the green grass across from the L. Street Bath House. With support of South Boston's State Senator Joseph Moakley, formal approval for the land was being sought with the Metropolitan District Commission (MDC). Due to the friction between political parties, two years had gone by since Senator Moakley had submitted our request for approval without any response. I recall that folks were very disappointed and wondered what was taking so long. It was Saint Patrick's Day, when both Democrats and Republicans put away their differences and celebrate at Dorgan's Restaurant on Columbia Road at the corner of G. Street. The event was chaired by the current State Senator Moakley. As Chairman of the Committee, I asked Joe Moakley what was taking so long. He pointed to the MDC Commissioner and said, "Ask him". I introduced myself and told the Commissioner how upset the residents of South Boston were with the delay about the statue of Father Joe. To my surprise he told me our request would be approved. Two weeks later it was approved. Next step was to select a day and plan for the dedication. As chairman of the committee, I notified Bishop Minihan, Father Joe's mother, his aunt, Senator Moakley, Representative Bulger, local politicians and local clergy. Again, Father Paul White was a great help in the planning and organization. The actual day of the dedication was a great success with Bishop Minihan and others giving tributes to Father Joe. Treasurer Jack Dever unveiled the statue, which was the most poignant moment of all and a day I will never forget.

Mrs. Laporte (glasses and hat), her cousin Margaret Hayes and
Humphrey Williams Sr at dedication of statue, April 21, 1968.

Southie Will Never Forget You

Jack Hurley

Jack Hurley, 2nd from left with friends

I was raised in South Boston and was 17 years old when I first met Father Laporte while he was assigned to Saint Monica's Parish. I was sitting in the back seat of a friend's car with three other friends when the back door opened and I heard a voice saying, "move over." Suddenly a priest got into the back seat introducing himself as Father Laporte of Saint Monica's Parish. He asks if anyone wanted to go to confession. I never forgot that moment, for I knew at that moment that he was a special priest. I recall he was ordained by the Archbishop of Boston Cardinal Richard Cushing on February 2, 1959. Father Joe, as we called him, did not spend a lot of time in one place. He was on the move all the time; he had to be---how else could he touch so many lives in the six short years he was in South Boston. What stands out the most about

Father Joe

Father Joe was his hearing our confessions outside the confessional. My friends and I would be hanging on a street corner, and he would stop by and ask if anyone wanted to go to confession. He would also hear confessions on the beach and within the L Street Bath House. I also remember the many bus trips he would organize to Hampton Beach, New Hampshire for the day.

It was in 1963 when I learned that he was ill and had been diagnosed with leukemia. During this time, I graduated from South Boston High School and enlisted in the United States Navy. Upon my discharge from the Navy, I returned home and learned that Father Laporte had been transferred to Gate of Heaven Parish in Southie.

Subsequently, in March of 1965 he succumbed to leukemia and died. I don't remember a lot about his funeral, and I don't think I want to. I lost a good friend.

Prior to Father Joe's death, I remember attending the dinner honoring him on September 27, 1964. The committee put together a 4-page newspaper that was distributed that evening. It was a 'tribute edition' titled "Father Joe's Journal," and its front-page headline read, **"Haverhill and Southie are His Home Towns. Youth Honors Rev. Laporte"**. Never was there a headline so true, for WE, the youth of South Boston, made this tribute happen. I have saved the newspaper for the past 58 years and was happy to be able to share it with the author of this book. All the articles from that paper were written by fellow priests, nuns, and friends of Father LaPorte and gives the reader a look into his many fine qualities and describes how he inspired all those that he encountered.

23

TRIBUTE DINNER TESTIMONIALS

Author's note: The following testimonials were re-typed verbatim from the original newspaper that was presented to attendees at the Father Laporte Tribute Dinner on September 27, 1964.

Youth Honors Rev. Laporte

By Bob Monahan

Five years ago, a tall, agile, muscular man named Joe Laporte received the Sacrament of Holy Orders. He was one of many young men to be ordained that February day. But for him it was a little different. He was destined to make a tremendous impact upon a nearby community... South Boston. And he did.

Rev. Joseph Laporte has a mannerism that has won him countless friends, admirers and confidants. His calling card is a combination of things. It consists of a likeable grin... a twinkling in his eyes... understanding... sympathy.... humor... a wave of the hand... the patience to listen... the wisdom to advise. A truly remarkable man.

Father Joe, as he is called by most of us, made an immediate and favorable reaction upon teenagers. His magnetic-like charm drew them to his side. Father Joe is truly unique. So much so that Southie's younger set-mostly between 18 and 23 - wished to show their appreciation for his friendship and deeds by holding a testimonial dinner in his behalf. A bold move, but a pleasing and impressive one.

Father Joe has the touch to reach the young man and the girl.

This is perhaps his greatest asset. But then again, he has a way of winning over children, young parents, the middle aged, the widow and the feeble. A truly remarkable man, this Father Laporte. No one person seems to know the entire story behind this wonderful man. His activities and accomplishments are like a gigantic puzzle. You pick up a piece here and another there, but you never can put them all together.

Apparently, he works a 25-hour day. In his short span as a priest he has converted 53 persons. That alone is sensational. But there's so much more. The hundreds of kids he's smartened up...the lad who he talked out of committing suicide... the bleeding man he chased, captured and carried to a priest house for medical aid...the tremendous success of his work with Chi Rho. The list of events is long, impressive and seemingly endless.

Father Joe's first station was at St. Monica's. In a short time, he had a following like a shepherd. His first friends in that parish were a group of young men who called themselves the Red Wings. To Father Joe they were angels with dirty faces. He won them over quickly. Many members of that group were responsible for arranging his testimonial.

Father Laporte then came to Gate of Heaven. He didn't come into the parish a stranger. Most of the parishioners either knew him or had heard of him because he was truly a remarkable man.

Southie Will Never Forget You

Many priests are known in one section of their city or town. This doesn't apply to Father Joe. Members of South Boston's other parishes- St. Augustine's, St. Bridget's, St. Vincent's, and St. Peter and Paul's are aware of his presence. He's known as sort of a Pied Piper. He's here, he's there, he's everywhere.

Non-Catholics also are familiar with this man. If he knowns a person needs help, Father Joe doesn't ask for credentials. He'd assist a Protestant or a Jew as quickly as a Catholic. Guess you can say he has that Ecumenical air about him.

Many people are proud of their South Boston heritage. When they gather and sing, "Southie Is My Home Town," they mean it. Father Joe can sing that song and mean it, too. True, he was Haverhill born, but no one will deny him the right to say that Southie is his hometown.

Father Joe also is a tease. His best performance at this art occurred during the summer of 1963 while he was celebrating the 10 o'clock Mass at Gate of Heaven. It was a hot, humid, muggy morning. The temperature was in the 90's. Beads of sweat were the vogue of the day.

Father Joe ascended the pulpit, read the weekly announcements and the gospel (this was before the change in the Mass).

The congregation remained standing when he finished reading the gospel, knowing only too well that no priest would give a sermon on such a blistering day.

Father Joe didn't move. The congregation reluctantly (and that's an understatement) sat.

Father Joe

"I know this is a hot, sticky, muggy morning," said Father Laporte. "But I want to tell you a story." Numerous groans echoed throughout the church.

"This is the story about a priest who gave a long sermon on a hot, muggy day like this," he said. A guy in the back pew felt the sweat running down his back and whispered to his wife, "The heat's got this guy." Father Joe went on, "This priest talked and talked and talked on this hot Sunday morning. After Mass he met an old woman who said she liked his sermon. The priest asked, "Which passage did you like best?" The woman's reply was, "Your passage from the pulpit."

With that, which took less than a minute, Father Joe whirled from the pulpit with half a grin and a twinkle in his eye and continued the Mass.

Father Joe has the ability of being seen at more places in less time than seems possible. You can spot him outside the priest house and moments later he's walking along the Strand way with a bunch of teenagers. Then he's back at the corner of, "I and Fourth" chatting with adults and in a flash, he's playing with some kids in the boy's section of the L Street Bath House. You'll see him at Castle Island one moment and at Columbia Stadium the next. A remarkable man.

The man you see in the black garb trying to grab a pass in the Gaston Schoolyard is Father Joe. He's the same dark clad figure patting a youngster's head on Broadway; consoling a woman on "K," Street; telling a joke on Fourth Street, and entering the Boy's Club on Sixth Street. A truly remarkable man this Father Laporte.

Southie Will Never Forget You

A year ago, last March, Bob Cousy of the Celtics was honored at Boston Garden. While the great Cousy wept without shame, a voice which belonged to Joe Dillon of South Boston-bellowed, "We all love ya, Cooz." Those five words were simple, sincere, but so effective.

I think they should be bellowed again - if Mr. Dillon doesn't mind a slight alteration- because "We all love ya, Father Joe." You're truly a remarkable man.

Lest We Forget

By Rt. Rev. John P. Carroll

One of the islands of the South Pacific unknown to most of us two decades ago, but forever etched by the blood of our boys on the hearts of the American people is the now famous Guadalcanal. During the war in a secluded well-hidden corner of this dense steaming island there stood a crude mess hall, crude to the eyes of those accustomed to comforts of home, but a castle to the boys far away from home.

Over the entrance to this hall hung a brown belt, bloodied and faded – all that remained of the possessions of a gallant marine, who had made the supreme sacrifice. Over the belt was the arresting inscription, "Lest we forget," – a mute and silent reminder of the debt they owed to this comrade who had fallen in battle. Yes, even on Guadalcanal with the fury of fierce fighting only a few miles away, men had to be reminded "Lest they forget,"- because man has the happy faculty of forgetting ever so easily.

Somewhere along the way some sainted soul realized that on the one hand the ordinary human travels on the fuel of love and appreciation and on the other hand, caught up in the hustle and bustle of life, we forget. Thus, birthdays, anniversaries and testimonials were introduced---bloodied belts reminding us of debts owed, lest we forget. A tip of the hat to the lads and lassies of famed South Boston for remembering not to forget.

The youth in parish programs represent a tremendous investment of time, talent and money on the part of these priests. The stakes are high. Our hope is that the program will develop talents. A Chet Collier received his first taste for dramatics in the CYO program and today he is one of the nation's leaders in television work. A Dick Farrell, learned the rudiments of baseball at St. Mary's Parish, Brookline and last July he pitched in the All-Star game representing the Houston Colts. An Art Graham took his first toddling steps as an athlete at St. Ann's Parish in Somerville and this fall, he is one of the top football players in the nation.

Our hope too, is that the CYO program will establish Catholic habits and attitudes. You might have read about Dick Donovan of the Cleveland Indians a former CYO boy from Sacred Heart Parish in Quincy. I once asked Dick what his greatest thrill in baseball was, thinking it might possibly have been the year he was picked as the outstanding right-hander in the American League. Actually, Dick's greatest thrill was his assist in converting a teammate.

Another hope is that the CYO will help young people to discover their vocation in life. The CYO is basically a challenge for the girls to be other Mary's whether their steps take them into the convent or into their own home of tomorrow. With the boys, we hope that the image of Christ is being stamped firmly on them. Naturally, every priest is especially happy when a boy from the parish youth program discovers he has a vocation to the priesthood. It is a fact that the close contact with the priest youth director many times results in the flowering of a vocation. A Seminary Rector once told me that he could pin-point the parish having active youth programs by the number of boys from the parish in the Seminary. In my own life, this was especially true. Back in the late twenties, a selfless priest, now gone to his reward, Fr. Thomas Murphy did a tremendous job with youth in the Immaculate Conception Parish in Malden. Twenty-six boys from that program later became priests.

These were some of the hopes and dreams of Father Laporte as he worked with the youth of South Boston during the past few years. Basically, his role has been one of privilege. However, as always, privileges carry with them a price. He has paid it to the hilt in long hours of patient, tireless, painstaking work for youth. I know his contribution is best known to the good Lord. His basic reward will always be the youth, now better citizens of God and Country because of his influence. They will eternally line his memory lane whispering their eternal thank-yous. Maybe his role as a priest in youth work is best expressed in this little poem:

Golden Opportunity

"I took a piece of plastic clay, and idly fashioned it one day;

and as my fingers pressed it still, it bent and yielded to my will.

I came again when days were past the bit of clay was hard at last.

My early impress still it bore and I could change its form no more.

You take a piece of living clay, and gently form it day by day;

molding with your power and art a young boy's soft and yielding heart. You come again when years are gone It is a man you look upon;

your early impress still he bore, and you can change him never more."

Father Joe

Bishop Joins Southie Lads In Tribute

By Bishop Jeremiah F. Minihan

I was delighted when I heard the news of the testimonial which is being tendered to Father Laporte by his devoted and grateful friends-the youth of South Boston-to whom he has devoted and dedicated his labors, his interest and his love during his time among them at St. Monica's and Gate of Heaven Parishes.

I have known Father Laporte since he was a youngster and it was my privilege and honor to preach the sermon at his first Mass in our home parish of St. James in Haverhill. I watched him grow from a young, sturdy, enthusiastic and dedicated boy, to the noble priest of God whom we now cherish as a brother in Christ to his fellow priests and a devoted father in Christ to the people, particularly to the youth, entrusted to his care.

His devotion to his work, far beyond the call of duty, has won for him the sincere esteem and high regard of his brother priests and the respect and love and affection of those towards whom he has demonstrated his loving and fatherly interest.

I am happy to join in this well-deserved tribute and to pray for Father Laporte, as you do, many more happy, blessed and fruitful years in the service of his God, his country and his church.

His Former Teachers Have Fond Memories

By Sister Mary Paulina and Sister Mary Marjarita

We had the pleasure of teaching Father Laporte while he was attending St. James in Haverhill, MA. We find it even more pleasing today when we see him perform his priestly duties at Gate of Heaven.

As a young boy Father Laporte excelled in two subjects: Religion and music. His strong love of God was evident at an early age.

Father Laporte was an extremely talented tap dancer. He was his classroom entertainer. Many times, when we had visitors in the classroom-especially Father Lyons-Joe the tap dancer would give an outstanding performance. He seemed to project so much during his earlier days....an outstanding characteristic which he still retains.

Father Laporte's dancing talents will be long remembered by those of us who were affiliated with him at St. James. As a first grader he did an Irish dance in a play called, "Come Back to Erin." One St. Patrick's Day he was billed as "Joe the Irisher." He was a member of St. James cheer leading section and he used to perform in a dance routine called "Norma and Joe," with his cousin.

Father Laporte seldom had to be punished in school, but he was what you'd call a real boy and there were times when he had punished tasks. One of these tasks was working the soap winder which was nicknamed the Laporte Soap Factory.

Father Laporte was one of the brightest students in the first grade. Once he won a prize - a piece of candy – for knowing the word blue.

Throughout his stay at St. James, Joe Laporte displayed kindness and loyalty to all the Sisters and Priests. He showed courtesy to all and always was very eager to help others. We use to call him, "ever ready Joe." Sometimes we are forced to smile when we think of Joe Laporte and his soap factory.... his tap dancing and other incidents. But those are things of the past now and Father Laporte is a Priest of God. We admire him .... respect him and would love to see a thousand more like him. Joe Laporte is a fond memory of the past. Father Laporte is the present and the future. God bless him.

Haverhill's Loss Is Southie's Gain

By Fran Donovan

This feeling has been expressed many times by Haverhill's friends of Father Laporte when, following his ordination he received his first assignment in South Boston and not in the Acre of St James's Parish.

To Father Joe, however, the assignment was just what he had hoped for so he could return to the parishioners with whom he had worked while undergoing seminary training.

With a name like LaPorte moving into Southie was not an easy task, however, the "old blarney" from his mother's side was soon realized and Father Joe had found a home.

Following his graduation from Saint John's Seminary and ordination to the priesthood in 1959, Father Joe was assigned to Saint Monica's parish in South Boston and served there until May 20, 1963, when he was transferred to Gate of Heaven Parish, also in Southie.

Father Joe's first assignment in Southie also came as somewhat of a surprise to many of his seminarian friends who believed he was more suited for the windy city. As Father Joe relates it, his sermons at the seminary were oblivious to dinner bells.

Father Joe was born Sept. 15, 1932, son of Mr. and Mrs. Joseph E. Laporte. He lived with his family at residences on Summer Street and Marshland Street before moving to 9 Park Street about 12 years ago where his mother still maintains the family residence.

Mr. LaPorte died several years ago but his athletic

prowess still is remembered in Haverhill's sports circles.

Father Joe attended Saint James Grammar School in Saint James's parish and graduated in 1946.

Recipe For a Priest

This one was submitted by a sixth grader:

One part kindness;
1 part generosity;
1 part humor;
5 parts holiness;
1 part intelligence;
2 parts understanding;
1 part patience.
Sprinkle lightly with mistakes and add a dash of good sportsmanship.

Let simmer for five years in a moderately strict seminary.

Or make them all like Father LaPorte.

Father Joe

Always Could Count On Father Laporte

By Rev. Leo V. Dwyer

I've known Father Laporte since he was about five years old, dressed in a white suit, black curly hair, representing St. John the Baptist in the lead position of our First Holy Communion class at Salisbury Beach.

I got to know him intimately as a student at St. James High School while stationed there.

We took numerous trips together after he learned to drive a car. We were together very often and I always could count on him.

I advised him to become a priest which he finally decided to become. I tried to encourage him when he was in the seminary. He fulfilled all my expectations and God called him to be His priest.

He was assigned to St. Monica's parish where I had been a curate years ago. He listened to my advice and got among the youth on the street. He fulfilled that to the letter. May God grant him strength to fulfill his mission to the youth of South Boston.

Cardinal Salutes Father Laporte

By Richard Cardinal Cushing

I am happy to add my greeting to those of the friends of Rev. Joseph E. Laporte. It is always a source of joy to me when the apostolic efforts of our wonderful Boston priests are recognized publicly.

In a world which pays small notice to spiritual values, the work of a priest is a matter of little concern. To those who are enriched with the gift of faith, however, it is a blessing which the Lord has sent. For as long as God wills it, the anointed hands of the priest are raised in benediction. His very presence is a joy to the young, a comfort to the aged, a consolation to the sick and dying. To the uninstructed he preaches and teaches the truths of eternal life. To the sorrowful sinner he speaks words of kindness, understanding and forgiveness. He is all things to all people, seeking nothing beyond the good of souls and looking towards no one but Christ to Whom he consecrates his energies and his whole being.

I am pleased to salute Father Laporte on this happy occasion. He has applied himself diligently and unselfishly to the service of the Church and the care of souls. He is a typical Boston priest who is loved and respected by people because of what he is and what he does.

May God bless, protect and reward him in His own inimitable ways.

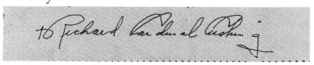

Father Joe

In the Seminary He Was...a Dark-Haired Whirlwind!

By Rev. A. Paul White

On a beautiful fall day in 1954, I encountered for the first time a six foot one, 195 pound dark-haired whirlwind who introduced himself as "Joe Laporte, from Haverhill." It was noticeable even then that he never walked anywhere. He rushed. And whenever you went with him from one building to another on the Seminary campus, you had the feeling of flight from some speedy, relentless pursuer. Here was a man in a hurry and if you would call him friend, speed became your constant companion.

Yet if there happened to be a fellow seminarian who injured a foot or was compelled by some physical necessity to walk slowly, Joe Laporte could be seen meandering along with him as though his most pressing problem consisted in placing one foot slowly ahead of the other.

Consideration for and understanding of people were among his most notable characteristics. He was very popular with his classmates and a genuine joy to be with. You left a conversation with Joe Laporte a happier person for having talked with him.

After his ordination, Father Laporte brought these characteristics to St. Monica's parish in South Boston. I am certain that many a St. Monica parishioner can testify from personal experience to these priestly traits that are so inextricably a part of Father Laporte.

His sense of humor is perhaps best illustrated by a story, (probably fictional), told about him. It is alleged to have occurred in a class conducted by a particularly stern seminary professor. About a week before class this professor had given Father Laporte a book of about 1700 pages to read and then pass on to his classmate. After he scanned this scholarly tome, he tried to give it to several of his confreres but they all avoided him and it. Finally, the week ended and the professor asked Father Laporte in class about the book and it's whereabouts. When Father Joe admitted that he still had it, the professor thought that he was enjoying it so thoroughly that he didn't want to pass it on and so he asked, "What impressed you most about the work?" And Father Laporte, recalling the 1700 pages he had been trying to unload for several days, answered: "It's weight, Monsignor." The reply of the professor has never been recorded.

While the story may not actually have happened, Father Laporte's sense of humor is real enough as all who have come in contact with him during his years in South Boston can readily testify.

I think that the priestly work performed so zealously by Father Joe has been most brilliantly epitomized by a French writer, Lacordare, when he wrote: "To live in the midst of the world without wishing its pleasure; to be a member of each family, yet belonging to none; to share all sufferings; to penetrate all secrets; to heal all wounds; to go from men to God and offer Him their prayers; to return from God to men to bring pardon and hope; to have a heart of fire for charity and a heart of bronze for chastity; to teach and to pardon, console and bless always, My God, what a life! And it's yours, O Priest of Jesus Christ."

Father Joe

Work With Chi-Rho a Great Success

By Rt. Rev. John T. Powers

We hear a great deal these days about young people — their likes and dislikes, hopes and fears, their problems and solutions. We know that they are interested in the Beatles, folk music, contemporary Jazz, hootenannys, the Twist, the Watusi and many other, what seem to us, musical aberrations.

In politics, they express concern about conservatism, liberalism, the John Birch society, civil rights, the Peace Corps, poverty, the coming elections. They wonder too about the Second Vatican Council, participation in the Mass, the question their vocation in life, their education — what kind, how much-- and the deepening of their spiritual commitment.

Youth then has many interests and of course this is true of our own sometimes maligned South Boston young people. Yet whenever we think of South Boston and youth, inevitably there comes to mind a flashing black-clad figure in the midst of them — our beloved Father Laporte. Whenever young people gather - on a corner, at a dance at a ball game, or Kelly's Landing- wherever they are — there he is. He cares about them, shares their enthusiasm and their problems — and they know it.

Here at Gate of Heaven Parish, Father Laporte began the Chi-Rho organization for young people aged 18 and over. This club takes its name from the first two letters of the Greek word for Christ, Our Lord. This organization tries to provide a worthwhile leisure time program for young people. It is designed to develop the talents of its members while instilling in them the true spirit of sportsmanship, a proper sense of values and a love of God and neighbor through Christian philosophy and teaching. To implant in our youth a sincere faith in God, a sound love of our country and a lasting faith in themselves — these are the purposes for which the Chi-Rho exists. Since its inception, the Gate of Heaven Chi-Rho has enjoyed a ski trip to New Hampshire, an outing at Sunset Lake outside Worcester and shortly will travel to New York City to visit the World's Fair. Once a month they receive Communion and attend Mass together and conclude with a breakfast meeting to plan coming events. All of this has been accomplished under the able direction of Father Laporte. I am very grateful for this opportunity to pay public tribute to this remarkable priest of God.

Priestly Love For People

By Rev. John McCarthy

To appreciate means to put a value, to esteem someone or something. In appreciating the worth of Father Laporte many thoughts suggest themselves. His service to the Church, his dedication to Christ the High Priest; his priestly love for people; his untiring and ceaseless devotion to youth all merit valid recognition and worthy praise.

But these fields of accolade I leave to others. Rather, as a fellow townsman and as one who has experienced the treasured opportunity of sharing rectory life with him, I would write of him as belonging to a unique fraternity, the brotherhood of Catholic Priests.

There is not under the stars an intimacy more profound than the bond between one Catholic priest and another. It needs no coaxing, no prelude, no ritual. It is subject to no formality. There is no shadow or barrier between us, neither age, nor antecedents, nor nationality, nor color of skin.

Ours is a blunt, rough-hewn affection. It forgets to be polite. I can sit at his table without invitation; sit in his study and read his books before I have ever met him; borrow his money (if he has any) and his clothes (if they fit) with no security.

His home is my home; his fireside, my fireside; his altar, my altar. I can give him my confidence promptly and without reserve. We can disagree without offense, praise each other without flattery or sit silently and say nothing.

Singularly we go our ways in our priestly labors,

establishing no generation, each a conclusion of his name yet always companioning one another with a strange sympathy too tender to be called friendship, too sturdy to be called love, but which God will find a name for when he searches our hearts in eternity.

As a fellow priest I am fortunate to share this unique fraternity with one of the mold of Father Joseph Laporte.

NEWSPAPER ARTICLES

Southie Shows Its Gratitude to Fr. Laporte, a 'Swell Guy'

Monahan, Bob, The Boston Globe September 6, 1964

Several dozen South Boston athletes are planning on honoring a priest whom they believe is one of the greatest 'sports' they've had the pleasure of being associated with. The likable padre is Rev. Joseph Laporte, a curate at Gate of Heaven Parish. To the kids in Southie, he's known as "Fr. Joe". The athletes who range in ages from 17 to 24 will hold a testimonial dinner in his honor at Blinstrub's Village in Southie on September 27. Fr. Laporte, Haverhill born and stationed in South Boston the past 4 1/2 years at St. Monica's and Gate of Heaven made most of his contacts with the athletes at South Boston Stadium, Marine Park and 'L' Street Bath House's handball courts. A spokesman for the group told the reasons for the testimonial. "To start with, Fr. Laporte is one heck of a swell guy", he said. "He's done so much for the younger people in South Boston that we wanted to do something to show our appreciation. "No one member of the group gets credit for the idea. Just say we all thought of it at the same time". "Fr. Laporte will go out of his way at any time to help people. He's a priest and he is 32, but we feel that he is one of us. He's smartened up a lot of young guys with good advice and we will never forget it." "He's sort of hard to explain. He just has a certain way about him. He reaches people easily and wins them over right away. He's really great". Members of the committee include Chairman John Connolly, ex-Christopher Columbus football and hockey player; Ray Flynn, former Southie High and Providence College star now with the Philadelphia 76's; Jack Denver, former B.U. hockey player and president of the South Boston Youth Hockey League; Warren Toland, standout Chippewa's ball carrier; and Jimbo Daly, former singles and doubles handball champ at 'L' Street. Then there's Dom Gentile, NuWay Sweepers star; Bob Nichols, an end at B.U.; Charlie Ray, former Southie and Chippewa's quarterback and current Chip end, Bill Bilton. The list continues with people like Chip LaPlaca, Frank Welby, Fred Paterson, Joe Ryan and goes on and on and even includes numerous teenagers from Southie. Fr. Laporte, tall, dark-haired, and agile, is famous for the way he circulated around Southie with alacrity. In his 'spare time' he can be found near the handball courts at 'L' Street; swimming at the 'L' or the Boys' Club pool; teaching youngsters how to throw a baseball or on the receiving end of a pass in a school yard. Fr. Laporte has displayed an abundance of affection for Southie's youth, and they are reciprocating.

Father Joe

Father Laporte Appreciation Dinner Complete Sell Out

South Boston Tribune September 24, 1964

Rev. Joseph E. Laporte--known as 'Father Joe' to hundreds of his friends in South Boston—will be honored at a testimonial dinner at Blinstrub's Village on Sunday at 6pm.

When the tribune went to press this function was a complete sellout. The committee in charge stressed that only persons holding tickets will be admitted. The testimonial for Father Laporte was thought up by a group of teen-agers and young men who have been associated with him the last five years. Father Joe's first station after ordination was St. Monica's. Now his home base is Gate of Heaven, but he considers all of Southie his parish. Father Laporte made a deep impression upon the youth of South Boston. He became one of them. He played with them—prayed with them -- and stayed with them. Southie's youth made a bold move by planning this testimonial. They embarked on a difficult mission and accomplished it. Father Joe's main interest in South Boston has been the younger set. Their affection for him can't be put into words. To them Father Joe is a friend—confidant—advisor. To them Father Joe is a regular Joe. South Boston's junior, intermediate and senior citizens also have a deep admiration for this Priest of God. Featured speaker at the dinner will be Bishop Jeremiah F. Minihan, who, like Father Laporte, is a native of Haverhill. Other head table guests include Rt. Rev. John T. Powers, Rt. Rev. Daniel J. Golden, Rev. John J. McCarthy, Rev. William F. Donovan, Rev. A. Paul White, Rev.

Southie Will Never Forget You

William G. O'Brien, Rev. Leonard T. McGrath, Rev. John P. Kelly, John Connolly, Jack Dever, Warren Toland, Bob Monahan and –Oh! Yes, Father Laporte.

Father Laporte Will Conduct Services At Gate Of Heaven

South Boston Tribune, October 15, 1964

The week of October 25 will be observed as Young Adult Mission Week in South Boston, it was announced yesterday by the Rev. Joseph Laporte, assistant at the Gate of Heaven Church and spiritual director of the movement.

Mission services will be conducted for young adults of all South Boston parishes at Gate of Heaven Church from Sunday October 25, through Thursday October 29.

Richard Cardinal Cushing has again endorsed this Mission and urges all young adults of high school and college age to attend the mission services each evening.

The theme of Mission Week which was inaugurated most successfully three years ago at St. Monica's Church by Father Laporte, will be: "The youth of today are the adults of tomorrow; they should prepare to accept their responsibilities in making a better world."

Further particulars on Young Adults Mission Week will appear in next week's edition of the Tribune.

Southie Will Never Forget You

Cardinal Cushing Endorses Young Adult Mission Starting Sunday

South Boston Tribune October 22, 1964

His Eminence Richard Cardinal Cushing this week gave enthusiastic endorsement to the Young Adult Mission which opens on Sunday evening in the Gate of Heaven church under the direction of Rev. Joseph Laporte. In a letter to Father Laporte the Cardinal said: "I am happy to learn of your Annual Mission for Young Adults. This is a grand spiritual project that could be imitated by all parishes throughout the Archdiocese. I pray that many will follow the example that you have established years ago. Please give all the Young Adults who will participate in the program my love, blessings and prayerful mementos. My one regret is that it is absolutely impossible for me to rearrange my program so that I could be with them at least one night during the mission. I urge all the parents of Young Adults to see to it that their sons and daughters participate in this Mission. It is an opportunity that should not be neglected. Begging God's choicest blessings upon you and with a prayer that you are keeping in good health, I am with special blessings and a pledge of prayerful mementos to all those who participate in the Mission.

Yours fraternally in Christ,

Richard Cardinal Cushing, Archbishop of Boston."

Mission services will be conducted on Sunday through Thursday, evening at 7:30 o'clock, closing with an evening mass on Thursday. Father Laporte's talks will deal with the problems of Young Adults in the World today. Father Laporte says, "Young adults in the United States now total more than the combined population of Chile, Sweden, and Uganda. These 22,505,000 young adults represent a tremendous reservoir of God-given energy, idealism and talent, every bit which is urgently needed in meeting the serious challenge of today and tomorrow. The Mission at the Gate of Heaven Church during the coming week will help prepare the young adult to face these challenges."

Gate Of Heaven Chi Rho Opens Second Season

South Boston Tribune October 22, 1964

The Gate of Heaven CHI RHO, headed by the Rev. Joseph Laporte, has started its second successful season. The CHI RHO (young adults) club has become the largest and most active club in the entire Archdiocese. Membership has doubled within the first year. The opening activity of the season was a hayride at the Lazy S Ranch in Canton, which proved to be a most enjoyable evening. During the past weekend Father Laporte and 52 members of the CHI RHO accompanied by Mr. and Mrs. George and Joseph Walsh visited the World's Fair. The next activity will be the Halloween Masquerade Party on Friday, October 30 at the Officers Club in the Fargo building. Prizes will be awarded for the best and most original costumes. Election of officers will take place on Sunday at Gate of Heaven Hall.

Father Joe

Father Joe: A Legend Dies, Southie Won't Forget

The Boston Globe March 15, 1965

Rev. Joseph E. Laporte, 32, who was assigned by Cardinal Cushing to "look after" the youth of South Boston, died late Saturday night after a two-year battle with leukemia. "Father Joe" was a priest for six years and the Haverhill native was stationed at St Monica's and Gate of Heaven in South Boston. He called himself "an adopted son of Southie". Father Joe's specialty was dealing with teenagers and young adults. And he didn't limit his services to Catholics. He also helped and earned the respect of Protestants and Jews. He was a tall, dark, handsome man and always didn't go by the book. He'd hear a boy's confession in a car or while walking along the beach. He'd instruct youngsters while attired in a bathing suit at the 'L' Street Bath House. Last Sept. 22 a group of young adults ran a testimonial to him at Blinstrub's. The event was so successful that hundreds couldn't get in. When Father Joe was introduced that night—although he didn't need an introduction---a group of young men bellowed, "We all love ya, Father Joe."

Less than two weeks ago Father Joe and Gate of Heaven basketball players were being fitted for jackets. The man who was taking the measurements asked the priest if he'd take off his suit coat. Father Joe obliged. The man said, "Father, you have a wonderful body. You must have been an athlete. You're a lucky man." Father Joe, who had been hemorrhaging for two days, smiled and said, "That's me. The lucky priest with the muscles". Two hours later he was hospitalized.

Southie Will Never Forget You

A few months ago, Father Laporte could have asked for and obtained a soft job which would give him more time to rest. He refused saying, "I have too much work to do, it will be a cold day in you know where when I quit."

He leaves his mother, Mrs. C. Evelyn (Williams) Laporte of Haverhill. A Children's Mass will be celebrated Thursday morning 8 am in Gate of Heaven Church, South Boston. The Office of the Dead will be chanted Thursday at 10 in Gate of Heaven Church, followed by a Pontifical solemn high Mass at 10:20. Burial will be in St. James Cemetery, Haverhill.

Mass Thursday for Fr. Laporte

The Haverhill Gazette March 15, 1965

A Pontifical solemn high mass will be celebrated Thursday morning at 10:20 at Gate of Heaven Church, South Boston for the Rev. Joseph E. Laporte, 32, son of Mrs. Joseph E. Laporte, 50 Eighteenth Ave., who died Saturday night at 11:45 at New England Baptist Hospital, Boston, a victim of leukemia.

Described by Richard Cardinal Cushing as one of the "most zealous and devoted priests he has ever known." Fr. Laporte knew of his illness for more than two years. He was doing well fighting back against the weakness, until he hemorrhaged badly two weeks ago and was hospitalized. From the pulpit of his church, it was requested that no more telephone calls or visits be made to the hospital. It was one of the few times anyone could remember a hospital patient who has too many people inquiring for him.

A children's Mass will be celebrated Thursday morning at 8 at Gate of Heaven Church by the Rt. Rev. John T. Powers, pastor. The Office of the Dead will be chanted Thursday morning at 10. Bishop Jeremiah F. Minihan, who preached the sermon at Fr. Laporte's first Mass, and was principal speaker at his testimonial, will celebrate the Pontifical funeral Mass at 10:20. The Rev. William G. O'Brien, assistant at St. Monica's Church, will be deacon, and the Rev. A. Paul White, assistant at Gate of Heaven, will be sub-deacon. The Rev. John C. Walsh, assistant at Sacred heart Church, Lynn, will give the eulogy. Burial will be in St. James Cemetery. Calling hours at the home of his mother, 50 Eighteenth Ave., will be anytime after 6 tonight, and anytime Tuesday afternoon. Calling hours at Gate of Heaven Church will be 6 to 10 Wednesday night. He is survived by his mother.

Father Joe

He Loses to Leukemia Southie Loved Fr. Joe

Sullivan, Tom , March 14, 1965 Source unknown

The priest who never gave up on his South Boston flock, despite the ravages of leukemia, died last night at New England Baptist Hospital. Only six years out of St. John's Seminary, 32-year-old Rev. Joseph E. Laporte succumbed to a disease which, for the past three years, he knew was closing in on him. He was fighting back against it and giving all of his time and energy to his friends, when he hemorrhaged badly 12 days ago and was hospitalized. As his life slowly ebbed, the people who knew and admired him deeply exchanged these observations in sidewalk conversation: "He's really a great guy, it's kind of hard to explain...Talking to him is just like talking to one of your own...He gave my mother the last rites and then she got better, so we used to call him 'The Healer'." He came to St. Monica's in South Boston six years ago, a Haverhill native just out of St. John's Seminary and he had nearly four good years there, a whirlwind working a 24-hour day, assisting the aged, converting 53 non-Catholics, but always concentrating on help to the young. After he became ill, he was transferred to Gate of Heaven Church, also in South Boston. Too sick for full-time duty, he specialized in the young men from mid-teens to mid-20's. This is how Fr. Joe fitted with his young flock: He would play football and baseball with them or go for a swim. But he was always a priest, aware of what he had to do for them. On a Saturday night, he would drive around the district. When he saw a group of young fellows on a street corner, he would pull up and tell them, "All right, fellows, one at a time." Then he would sit in the backseat of his car and hear their confessions. There was a magnetism about him that broke down the rebellious attitude of many wild young people toward authority. From the pulpit, it was requested that no more telephone calls or visits be made to the hospital. It was one of the few times anyone could remember a hospital patient who had too many people inquiring for him. Last September, when the young people got together to show him how grateful they were, a four-page newspaper was published with the financial help of 22 organizations, including Chippewas, the Daffy Doodlers and the L Street Bath House Employees. One headline read: "We All Love Ya, Father Joe." Cardinal Cushing wrote: "He has applied himself diligently and unselfishly to the service of the Church and the care of souls. He is a typical Boston priest who is loved and respected by people because of what he is and what he does. May God bless, protect, and reward him in His own inimitable way." Southie is a warm-hearted place. Father Joe is basking in that warmth right now.

Father Joe

Pontifical Mass At 10 O'Clock

South Boston Tribune March 18, 1965

Solemn funeral services for the Rev, Joseph E. Laporte , South Boston's beloved "Father Joe" and apostle to teenagers will take place this morning in the Gate of Heaven Church with the Office of the Dead being chanted at 10 o'clock by members of the diocesan clergy, followed by a solemn pontifical Mass at 10:20. Most Rev. Jeremiah Minihan, Auxiliary Bishop of Boston, will be the celebrant of the Mass, assisted by the Rev. William G. O' Brien, curate at St. Monica's Church; deacon; Rev A. Paul White, curate at Gate of Heaven Church, sub-deacon. The eulogy will be preached by Rev. John C. Walsh, curate at Sacred Heart Church, Lynn. Rt. Rev. John T. Powers, pastor of gate of Heaven Church, will celebrate a children's Mass at 8'oclock this morning. Units in the Evacuation day parade paid a special tribute in passing Gate of Heaven Church yesterday, with bands performing dirge music and military bodies rendering the salute. Father Laporte was a chaplain in the Army Reserve.

Lying-in-state took place last evening following the parade with thousands of persons from all parts of the city visiting the church to pay a last farewell to the beloved priest. Father Laporte, who died of leukemia late Saturday at the New England Baptist Hospital, was a native of Haverhill. He graduated from St. James High School in the city in 1950. He studied for the priesthood at St. John's Seminary, Brighton, and was ordained in February 1959, by Richard Cardinal Cushing. His first assignment was to St. Monica's parish.

Southie Will Never Forget You

Father Laporte is survived by his mother, Mrs. Catherine Laporte of Haverhill. Burial will be in St. James Cemetery, Haverhill. During his short priestly life, all of which was spent "looking after the youth" of South Boston, Father Laporte was prodigal in his efforts to improve the spiritual, moral and physical well-being of young people here. His methods with the young, which some might have thought unorthodox, were effective, as were evidenced by the success of the Young People's Mission which he conducted for the past two years and the revitalizing of the Chi Rho movement in this section. He was chaplain of the South Boson Little League and took an active interest in the work of the Babe Ruth and Connie Mack baseball leagues. Father Laporte's work for the youth of the district was publicly recognized when youth itself sponsored a testimonial in his honor last September at Blinstrub's, an event that saw one of the greatest gatherings in recent South Boston history. He has been the subject of many tributes in recent days, including several appearing in this edition. Summing up, The Tribune, would reiterate the statement of its Newscope columnist: "It would have been un-American not to like Father Joe."

Father Joe

In Memoriam Patris Juvenae

South Boston Tribune March 18, 1965

Rev. Joseph E. Laporte
R.I.P.

It was a dark, cold night as a housekeeper at the Gate of Heaven rectory answered the bell to find a worn, tattered figure on the doorstep. The woman, obviously troubled, asked, "Is Father LaPorte in?" The answer was immediate for Father LaPorte was always available: "Yes. Please step in here and Father will be with you presently." An hour later a different woman emerged from the room. Her face had lost its gloom and her figure had been given new life through the injection of hope she had received. Then, not elated but stronger in her faith, she left for home. Father LaPorte then emerged, as tall and vital as ever, but, if one were to look closely enough into his dark eyes, he would see their luster had been dimmed one more degree as he took the woman's problems to his heart and made them his own. He went to his room, to sit and ponder those things known only to a priest. He had, since his arrival in "Southie" a scant 6 years ago, brought a new life, a new spirit, a new vitality to this old neighborhood. He took its youth and channeled their drives, ambitions and energies into those directions which would make them better young men and women, better fathers and mothers, better citizens of their city, state, country and of the world. He comforted the aged in their last hours and he gave consolation to families in times of sorrow. He bound together all components of the community and made out of the many, one. Now he has reached his goal, the goal for which we all strive. He is in the House of his Father and we are better for his having been here. "Oh God... mercifully grant that we may imitate his example."

This tribute to our late, beloved friend was written by one of Father LaPorte's many friends among the student body at South Boston High School and is published anonymously that it might better stand for us all.

Father Joe

He Was My Friend

Casper, Joe, South Boston Tribune March 18, 1965

Rev Joseph LaPorte, who died on Saturday, lives in the hearts of young people of all ages. How could anyone who knew him as a priest and a person ever forget him. His familiar happy greeting, "Hey, how's it going Joe?" will ring in my ears the rest of my life. Father Joe deeply concerned with the futures of young people, and he extended every effort to be available whenever the need arose. He once said in a talk that I attended, "We must find ways to help young men and women who haven't conformed to society, to feel wanted, to feel that there is always room for them." I ran into Father Joe a couple of affairs in a row and kiddingly said to him, "Are you here again?" He said, "You know me Joe, I'll go anywhere for a free meal!" The touching tribute which was extended in his honor on September 27 at Blinstrub's Village before a "standing room only" crowd was magnificent. It was a tender way of saying how very much his presence has meant to the people of South Boston. Father LaPorte could get more boys into one car than any man I have ever seen. I once asked him how he felt and almost bit my tongue for having let the question slip out. He said, "Joe, the doctors told me I could live a year or ten years, but in life we never have any way of knowing. God has been good to me. He knows what is best." Father Joe had the ability to talk to a person in a crowd and make them feel as if he and they were the only two people around. His youth missions were always well received by the teenagers of the district. He was as manly a person as anyone I have ever met. Never once had I talked with him and not felt better after the conversation. He was one of the busiest men I know, and yet he always had time. This morning at the Gate of Heaven Church, thousands will bid farewell to their friend, Rev Joseph LaPorte. Each one in his heart will join together in remembering his friendship and some cherished moment which they spent with him. At the hospital he said, "I know that I'm going; it's God's will, but I feel so sad that my mother will be left all alone." The memory of his presence is so vivid that it seems as though he is only being transferred to another parish. In essence this is so, for wherever there is a need, those of us who have been touched by his presence will feel encouraged. If he were here now, he would be saying, as he had before, "Joe, please, you're embarrassing me, stop writing all those nice things." Father Joe is one-person about whom I can honestly say, I have never heard anyone say a critical or unkind word. It would be un-American not to have liked him. Say a prayer for him and thank God for having sent him to us. Those who knew him are surely saddened but richer for having known him. He Was My Friend.

Author's note: In recent talks with Joe Casper, of Casper Funeral Services, South Boston, he recalled in the past most funeral directors in Southie, would ask families of the deceased permission to place flowers at the foot of the Fr. Joe statue. For years that practice continued to honor Southies beloved priest.

Father 'Joe' Laporte

Flanagan, Bill, South Boston Tribune, March 18, 1965

Two years at The Gate of Heaven, keeping our youth from sin,

Sent you to the gates of heaven, where St. Peter said, "Come in".

God has just made you a pastor, in a parish up above,

You earned your latest transfer, giving children six years of love.

No more confessional hearings, on sidewalks or in cars,

Now you're watching all our actions, from up there amongst the stars.

Somebody up there loves you, so a special delivery letter,

Summoned you, to come and do, and make heaven a little bit better.

Dear Father Joe, you had to go, God always has the preference,

Our Southie youth told our Lord the truth when he asked them for a reference.

So, on the seventeenth of March, as your body lies here in state,

We know your soul is with St. Patrick's, inside that other gate.

Letters To The Editor

South Boston Tribune March 18,1965

Editor of the Tribune:

All Southie mourns for the beloved Father Laporte. We, in Old Harbor Village, have a very special place in our hearts for him. Many words. Spoken and written, will go forth in his memory. But it is the unspoken words of the love in our hearts that can never really be expressed. Holy Mother Church says it for us, "The just man shall be an everlasting remembrance and an evil report he shall not fear."

Sincerely, "The Neighbors on O'Callaghan Way"

Thousands Mourn 'Fr. Joe'

Negri, Gloria, The Boston Globe March 18, 1965

You had to notice inside the Gate of Heaven Church Wednesday night that it was the children- the children with the patched up clothes and the old-young faces-who bent closest to his casket, as if to kiss his cheek. You had to notice that the hands that reached out to lightly touch his hand, his shoe, or the lace of his priest's vestments, were mostly young hands to whom death is no stranger. "My father died two Februarys ago and Fr. Joe came to see him, even though he didn't know him," a 10-year-old from South Boston said, tears welling in his eyes. "Fr. Joe"- Rev. Joseph E. Laporte, curate at Gate of Heaven Church in South Boston for the last two years-came home to his flock Wednesday night.

Dead of leukemia at 32, Southie's beloved "Fr. Joe" had been brought from his mother's home in Haverhill to lie in state among the people he has loved and cherished for the last five years, first at St. Monica's, then at Gate of Heaven.

Thousands streamed through the big yellow-brick church on East Fourth St. from the time Fr. Joe's body arrived at 6 p.m. until the church closed at midnight. They were like subjects paying homage to a beloved king death had taken from them.

"If you only knew what he was like," sobbed Mary Doran of East Third St. "He was a living saint. I've been in this parish 50 years and there's never been anyone like him."

"Just what he did for the kids. That's enough for a book. And if any of them had any bad action about them, he changed their whole lives. Look at them come...look at them come."

Hundreds of Fr. Joe's kids came to bid their last farewells Wednesday night. Many of them were good kids—Fr. Joe was the last man who'd admit there was such a thing as a bad kid. Some of them were kids who might have gone wrong if it hadn't been for Fr. Joe. Some of them had been bailed out of court by Fr. Joe.

"I guess the only thing we can do now is try to be good like Fr. Joe wanted us to," one of them said.

Fr. Joe's casket lay in the center aisle near the altar where two Masses—one a Children's Mass—will be said for him today. He wore his Mass vestments—the purple chasuble for mourning. The Rosary was wound around his folded hands. Six tall candles flickered along the sides. Those who had known Fr. Joe said he seemed to be smiling a bit—"just like he always was," 14-year-old Jimmy Moynihan of Dorchester Ave said. Jimmy watched the throngs pay their respects.

"I think maybe Father Joe had too many friends," Jimmy said. "He used to work day and night. He never got any sleep. Why, Monsignor Golden said at church Sunday that "Father Joe did the work of 10 priests." Rt. Rev. Daniel Golden is pastor of St. Monica's.

Why do all the kids love Father Joe so much? Jimmy was asked.

"He was a father to all us kids," Jimmy said. "If you were really bad, Father Joe would do half your penance for you.

"If Father Joe saw one of us kids smoking, he'd joke that the next time he caught us at it, he would make us eat the cigarette. And I believe he would have, but only because he didn't want us to start smoking and get tough."

McCarthy, George Our Father LaPorte

The Supreme Digest of the Supreme Diner and Restaurant 274 Southhamptom Street, Boston, Mass. March 18, 1965.

"Any coward can fight a battle when he is sure of winning: but give me the man who has pluck to fight when he's sure of losing." I can't remember just where I saw this quotation, but this was Father LaPorte's creed. He came to us here in South Boston six years ago. St. Monica's parish is where he started his life's work. Young, vigorous, and happy, this man of God reached out to youth. Denounced, hammered from all sides, the teenager's image today is a poor one. Father Laporte thought otherwise. Here in South Boston, we, like every other part of our great cities had and have, a number of teenage wildcats. Father Joe Laporte was certain he could tame them. No street in Southie was unknown to him. It was never too early or too late to find him somewhere with a group of youngsters. It had to be the infinite wisdom of Almighty God who gave this man to us. Perhaps he had been forewarned because he filled the twenty-four hours of each day with a labor of love. He became a living symbol for our youth. If truth and decency and self-respect needed more light, Father LaPorte stood by. About two years ago doctors told this man that the illness he had contracted left him with only a short time. He could have stopped right there, retired to a bed in a hospital and quietly waited for his time to come. Surely no one would have censored him for this. He had other plans, however, the first one was to keep on going as long as his waning strength would last. This is what he did. He knew and we knew that his sun was slipping ever westward and soon would dip beneath the far horizon. Never before have I met a man who could and did in fact face eternity and laugh. Where did he find this well of courage, did he know there was a place waiting for him beside his God? Now he has gone and we have lost a voice who spoke with calm, with hope, and understanding. The boys he knew, the good and bad, can't forget. For some of them he pledged his word and the law saw fit to believe him. The walls of a prison can break a boy and Father LaPorte knew this. Today, now, if there is just one young man who fell within the shadow of wrong and asked Father LaPorte for help and received it without any reservations, multiply this by one hundred. The last time I talked with him was when some of my football team, along with myself, dropped into the rectory up at Gate of Heaven Church. We wanted him to draw a ticket for our Jacket Fund. He did. The first-time I met him he was smiling, the last time I saw him he was smiling, joking with the kids. This past year may have been a difficult one for him because I could see the almost imperception strain on his face. If there was a sadness in him, it was only because he could not finish the job he started out to do. There was so much to do and so little time left to him. Perhaps it was a bit too much to ask him to keep this man among us for years to come. I don't believe we need to build a memorial of stone to Father LaPorte because the wind and rain and time would tarnish it. He is safe and warm and ever living in the hearts and minds of every boy and girl he ever walked with. They call us tough and hardboiled here in South Boston but really, we're not. We know heartbreak and what it means to lose someone you love. I'm thankful that in my lifetime I can say with honest pride that Father Laporte was my friend, too.

St. Monica's Sports Night Tomorrow Proceeds to Aid Memorial to Late Father Laporte

South Boston Tribune May 6, 1965

St. Monica's Holy Name Society will present an Evening of Sports tomorrow night at 8 o'clock in St. Monica's auditorium, Old Colony Avenue and Preble Street. Program Chairman Walter Shannon, Jr., and Harold Whitcraft have lined up a fine evening of entertainment for all. Admission is 50 cents. Proceeds will benefit the "Father Joe Memorial" in memory of the late Rev. Joseph Laporte. Society President James M. Collins and Ticket chairman Tom Kane remind all that the drawing of prizes for the Fr. Joe Lectern subscription will take place at this Sports Nite. If you have yet to make your returns, please do so at the rectory or bring them to the Sports Nite. Anyone desiring more subscriptions books please call Jim Collins at TA 5-9314. "Do your share; make this project a huge success in memory of Father Joseph Laporte. Come to the Sports Night Friday," President Collins says.

Chi Rho Plans Sports Night Here

South Boston Tribune May 19, 1965

The Gate of Heaven Chi Rho will hold a sports night next Wednesday, May 19th, in the parish hall, E. Fourth and I Street.

Proceeds from the event will go towards the establishment of a memorial to the late Rev. Joseph Laporte.

The program will include color sound sports films, including the 1964 Olympics. Autographed World Series baseballs and bats will be raffled. Admission is free and all adults and children of the district are invited to help in establishing a lasting memorial to Father Laporte.

Father Laporte Memorial Committee Will Hold Meeting This Evening

South Boston Tribune August 5, 1965

Statues, Scholarships Among Proposals Already Received

The Father Laporte Memorial Committee will meet this evening at 8:30 o'clock in Gate of Heaven Hall to discuss suggestions for memorial remembrances to the late beloved priest who was known as South Boston's "Apostle to Youth." Memorial suggestions already received by the committee range from a bust or statue of Father Laporte to be erected at the intersection of Day Boulevard and L street to scholarships for local youth. Among suggestions received was that of renaming Dorchester Street as Laporte Avenue. Regarding this suggestion, Robert O'Brien of 151 H Street, chairman pro-tem of the memorial committee, stated yesterday that the committee to rename Dorchester Street is an entirely separate group. The purpose of the Father Laporte Memorial Committee is to select a fitting memorial to the late Father Laporte, excluding remaining Dorchester Street, since there is already a committee working towards that goal. Although several good suggestions have already been made, ideas are still being accepted, in order that every resident of South Boston may have the opportunity to suggest a fitting memorial to Father Laporte. Please send your suggestions to the Father Laporte Memorial Committee, care of Rev. Paul White, Gate of Heaven Rectory, 606 E. Fourth Street, South Boston, Mass, 02127

Fund-Raising Drive for Fr. Laporte Statue Starting Tomorrow

South Boston Tribune September 16, 1965

A house-to-house fund raising drive will be held in a large sector of South Boston (G to M streets, E. First street to Columbia Road) starting tomorrow to obtain contributions for the Rev. Joseph E. LaPorte, 'Father Joe', Memorial Fund. The drive, which will be conducted mostly by youths who were advised by the late priest, will continue over the weekend. All monies collected will be used to erect a statue in memory of Fr. Joe at 'L' street and Day Blvd. Persons who may not be home during the drive may make donations through the use of a coupon which will be found elsewhere on this page. Last week the following made donations... (*Author's note; For the sake of privacy, names, addresses and amount of money contributed has been omitted from this article*).

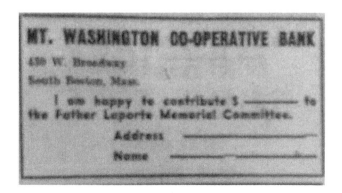

Father Joe

Fr. Laporte Committee Given Liberal Response To Appeal

The South Boston Tribune Thursday, September 23, 1965

The Father Laporte Memorial Committee, which began its house to house solicitation for contributions last week, has received a most heartening response in the first day of its campaign. Co-chairman John O'Connor and Robert Murphy are happy to report that cooperation with the committee has been excellent. Everyone was more than happy to contribute so that the people of South Boston will have a tangible, lasting memorial to Father Joseph Laporte. The sum already received by the fund now totals $2,231, which means that $7,759 is needed to achieve the goal of $10,000. Solicitation will continue tomorrow night in the City point section of the district. The committee urges all to be as generous as the contributors last week. Contributions may be mailed by using the coupon on page 1 of the Tribune and sending it to the Mt. Washington Co-operative Bank. A partial list of contributors in the first week of solicitation includes: Mrs. Laporte, $390.

(Author's note; For the sake of privacy, additional names, addresses and amount of money contributed has been omitted from this article).

Laporte Memorial Fund Passes Half-Way Mark

South Boston Tribune October 7, 1965

Co-Chairmen Ask More Volunteers for Solicitation

Contributions toward the erection of the Father Joseph Laporte Memorial Statue have not passed the halfway mark. As of Tuesday, the committee treasurer announced that total contributions are slightly in excess of $5,000, which is most heartening to all the young adults who have given so unselfishly of their time in recent weeks. However, with limited staff and resources of the fund committee, it is imperative that some assistance be forthcoming in the form of volunteer helpers on solicitation nights. If you can donate just one hour of your time on either Friday or Monday night at 6:30 o'clock, please be at Gate of Heaven parish hall on these evenings. The co-chairman of the committee believed that at this time it would be well to state the three-fold purpose which motivated the committee to decide on a statue of South Boston's beloved "Father Joe." The statue is seen as: 1) A tribute of thanks for Father Laporte's many accomplishments and kindnesses in the South Boston district, 2) a perpetuation of the Christian ideals which he so well conveyed to the youth of South Boston, 3) a debt of gratitude to all the priests, nuns, and ministers who have always given of their best for South Boston. *(Author's note; For the sake of privacy, names, addresses and amount of money contributed has been omitted from this article).*

Southie Team Dedicates Win to 'Father Joe'

The Boston Globe October 14, 1965

South Boston High quarterback Dennis Flynn said the football team tried to win Wednesday's game with Boston College High School for the late Rev. Joseph E. (Father Joe) Laporte. "We all agreed before the game that we'd try to win for Father Laporte', said Flynn. "We all knew him and liked him. He used to come to most of our practices". "After we won we went into the dressing room. We all knelt down and said a prayer for Father Joe." Father Laporte, who worked with the youth of South Boston, died last March.

Volunteers Are Still needed By Laporte Memorial Fund

South Boston Tribune October 21, 1965

People interested in helping to make the FATHER
LAPORTE MEMORIAL a successful venture should contact
Chairman Bob Murphy at AN 8-6903. After five weeks of
extensive soliciting the committee has barely reached the
halfway mark. The immediate need is that friends of the last
priest donate ONE HOUR of their time on any Friday night so
that they might help to perpetuate his memory. WILL YOU
add your NAME to the list of committee members??? If so, call
Bob. The committee would like to thank the following for their
generous donations and a special thanks to two youngsters (7
and 9) who have collected a total of $125.32. Thank you.
(*Author's note; For the sake of privacy, names, addresses and
amount of money contributed has been omitted from this article*).

Laporte Memorial Fund Lags Due To Lack of Solicitors

South Boston Tribune October 28, 1965

The Father Laporte Memorial Committee has collected $5,500 to date. This figure is just barely past the half-way mark. Collecting the additional amount to make this venture a success will be difficult unless the committee receives co-operation from a FEW of the late priest's young friends, who have yet announced their desire to aid in making this tribute a success.

WHERE HAVE THEY BEEN?

The task of collecting this large amount has been shared by a few of Father Laporte's friends who have not forgotten him. To be successful the committee needs the co-operation of all. Have you forgotten? If not, contact after 6 P.M. any person listed below. (*Author's note; For the sake of privacy, names, phone numbers and amount of money contributed has been omitted from this article*).

They Remember

O'Donnell, Richard W., The Boston Globe March 13, 1967

Father Laporte 'Practiced What He Preached'... 'He Belonged'... He Was One Heck of a Fellow'

An anniversary requiem Mass for the late Rev. Joseph E. Laporte will be sung at 7 this evening in the Gate of Heaven Church, South Boston.

Father Laporte died two years ago. But the memory of the man is as vivid today to the young people of South Boston as it was when he walked among them. The 32-year-old curate knew that leukemia was robbing him of his life. Rest would have helped. Instead, the priest chose to stay with his young friends until the very end.

"They still talk about him," said Rev. Paul White of the Gate of Heaven Church, who will officiate at the memorial Mass. "They loved Father Joe. Some of the older boys, who knew him when he was alive, are overseas in Vietnam. Whenever they write to us, they always mention "Father Joe." Father Joe, and that was what the youngsters of South Boston called him, was a Haverhill native. His mother, Mrs. C. Evelyn (Williams) Laporte, still resides there. Haverhill may have been the young priest's birthplace, but he considered himself, "an adopted son of South Boston". He was stationed at both Saint Monica's and Gate of Heaven in that district.

CONFESSION ON BEACH. He was a tall, dark and handsome man, and he did not always go by the book. He'd hear a boys confession in a car, or while walking along the beach. He'd instruct youngsters while attired in a bathing suit at the L Street Bath House. His priestly techniques may have been different, but they certainly were effective. Two years after his death, the young people still remember him. Said a young man in his early 20's: "I graduated from Boston College in 1965. I had no intention of going to college. But Father Joe kept at me." Another youth said, "I think his secret was that he was equally at home with the Cardinal or with a kid who was in a scrape." A 19-year-old City Pointer declared: "I never met a priest like Father Joe. He practiced what he preached." Said another boy: "He had a personal touch. He made you feel your friendship was the most important thing in the world. There'd be a card game and he'd be one of us. He was a kibitzer. He belonged." A teenager said: "If there was a break into a house or store, Father Joe knew who was responsible. He didn't go running to Station Six. He went to the boy to get him back on the right track again."

HECK OF A FELLOW. Perhaps, a young lad just approaching shaving age said it best, when he declared: "Father Joe was one heck of a fellow." Since his death, South Bostonians of all ages, and religions too, have been attempting "to build a suitable memorial for Father Joe." A fund-raising drive has been started. The money reportedly will be used to place a statue of the priest across the way from the L Street Bath House. Yet, in the final analysis, Father Laporte erected his own, "suitable memorial."

Southie Youths Remember Friend A Statue for Fr. Joe

Riddell, Janet, The Boston Globe April 22, 1968

FATHER LAPORTE'S MEMORIAL IN SOUTH BOSTON
... "he was one of the boys" (Bill Brett Photo)

Photo used with permission of Bill Brett

The way Jim Daley remembers, it was a chilly day in 1959, and the kids were slapping their fists into their leather mitts while waiting for some action on the baseball diamond at Columbia Park.

And while they were all standing there certainly not thinking much about church or religion, this tall dark-haired athletic-looking guy with a friendly grin ambled over to watch the game and afterwards started talking. That was the casual way Rev. Joseph Laporte introduced himself to the young people of South Boston.

On Sunday, some of those same young people dedicated a statue to the handsome priest who preached on the baseball field, the basketball court, and on the beach, before dying of leukemia in 1965 at 32.

Several hundred people were there in front of the L Street Bath House in South Boston to see the bronze statue of the priest unveiled—including Fr. Laporte's mother, Mrs. C. Evelyn Laporte of Haverhill and Most Rev Jeremiah F. Minihan, auxiliary bishop of Boston.

But most of all there were the young adults in their early and late 20's headed by Bob Murphy and John O'Connor, who began a door-to-door campaign three years ago to raise money for the Italian-made monument.

They remember Fr. Joe as a friend and confidant, as a guy who brought the church into South Boston streets and teen hangouts, and who in some cases changed their lives.

Jim Daly, 27, pointed across the street into the bathhouse, a popular hangout for Southie youth, and recalled that "Fr. Joe used to come down to the bathhouse to talk to the kids about their problems and he would go down to the beach in his bathing suit and hear boys' confessions as he walked along the waterfront."

Daly was a red-haired freckled kid of 18, working as a lifeguard and playing outfield for a local baseball team when he met the priest at Columbia Park. Now a teacher, Daly wasn't sure he wanted to go to college until he was talked into it by Fr. Laporte.

"He was just a regular guy—I guess you might say he was one of the boys," Daly recalled.

"Fr. Joe did everything," recalls 20-year-old Robert Taylor, a slim blond youth who met the priest playing basketball. "He used to go swimming with us and he'd play basketball with us."

"A lot of the time he didn't wear his priest suit or whatever you call the suit that priests wore ('Cassock' whispered one of Taylor's friends), but anyway he dressed like all of us, and he had confessions in his car and on the street corners and he was just always around. I don't think he ever slept." Almost every kid present for the unveiling Sunday seemed to have a story to tell about Fr. Laporte.

How the priest was playing basketball and accidentally knocked a fellow player who, not knowing he had been hit by a priest promptly swore at him and threatened a fight, and how the father invited the angry player for a hamburger and a frappe and subsequently brought him into the church.

How a kid stabbed another kid in a fight late at night and fled into the dark, later giving himself up—not to his parents or to the police, but to Fr. Joe.

How Fr. Joe walked up and down Day Blvd and knew every kid's name and how he stopped gang fights and had everyone from high school dropouts to young seminarians emulating him.

He met a kid named Greg McDermott on a basketball court and another kid named Mel Feeney on South Boston streets and encouraged both of them to enter the seminary.

Father Joe

He was stationed at St. Monica's and Gate of Heaven, but his parish was all of South Boston—including the gas station where a group of teenagers broke in one night to steal.

"The cops caught them and the first one they asked for was Fr. Joe," recalls Daly, adding that Fr. Laporte saw that the youths returned what they stole and soon had the would-be thieves attending worship services at his "Teen Mission."

The priest's life has inspired other young theologians, such as Tom Forry, who is scheduled to be ordained into the priesthood next month.

"Can you believe? He had these kids following him like the pied piper," says Forry. "I mean teens are tough. They don't want to talk about religion. But Fr. Joe spoke their language. He was like Christ. He was out with the people, out on the streets and in the projects. I could never match the guy. But I plan to work out in the streets--- not be afraid to hear confessions in cars---not be afraid to be radical."

600 Honor 'Father Joe" at Southie Dedication

Sullivan, Mary X., Record American April 22, 1968

Braving biting winds from the Atlantic Ocean, more than 600 South Boston residents gathered at L Street and Day Blvd, yesterday for the dedication of a statue in honor of 'Father Joe' whose motto was "Have confessional will travel". More than half of them were young people, who had been children or teenagers when Father Joseph E. Laporte came into their lives. These young people collected nearly $8,000 mostly in contributions of a dollar or two, to construct this memorial to a priest who was their friend and who died of leukemia in 1965 at the age of 32. Father Laporte was born in Haverhill, but after his ordination in 1959, when he was assigned first to St. Monica's and later to Gate of Heaven Church, Southie became his hometown and youth his apostolate.

Bishop Present Seldom have more sincere and heartfelt tributes been uttered on such an occasion. Among those who spoke on the windswept platform opposite the L Street Baths were two seminarians who had been "Fr. Joe's boys". Bishop Jeremiah F. Minihan, who like him, grew up in St. James Parish in Haverhill and the co-chairmen of the memorial fund, John O'Connor and Robert Murphy. The 187th Infantry Brigade of the Army was represented by Brigade Chaplain Ray Marshall and an honor guard and the South Boston community by members of the Legislature and City Council. Bishop Minihan paid tribute to Fr. Laporte's mother who was also present and who unveiled the statue. "Although from Saint James Parish there has come a long line of priests, Fr.

Father Joe

Laporte's vocation came not from the priests but from his home," he said.

Influenced Young One after the other told of Father Joe's influence on the young, on his hearing confessions in his car, in a gym, or wearing swim trunks on the beach. "Have confessions will travel," was his motto one speaker said.

The bronze statue executed in Italy by Sculptor A.J. Daprato depicts a slim young cassock clad priest whose hands rest on the shoulders of a young boy. This purely representational work of art would not please the modernists who prefer faceless and almost formless sculpture, but the people of South Boston would have scorned such a memorial. "You'd think he was going to open his mouth and speak to us. God love him" murmured a soft Irish-accented voice. This representational art... truly representative of a priest who will be long remembered.

Remembering Father Joseph Laporte Gate of Heaven

St. Brigid, St Monica-St Augustine Parishes Bulletin, March 15, 2015 (50th Anniversary of His Death)

Rev. Joseph Laporte, or "Father Joe", was Parochial Vicar at St. Monica Parish and Gate of Heaven Parish from his ordination in 1959 until his early death in 1965 at the age of 32. Fr. Joe was born in Haverhill but belonged in South Boston. He was ordained by Cardinal Richard Cushing on February 2, 1959, and sent to South Boston to "look after the youth." A parish history book from St. Monica published in 1980 stated: *Father Laporte especially made a tremendous impression on the young. Many remember how he would find youngsters on street corners and listen to their confessions or how he organized a special Devotional Mission for South Boston youths.* Newspaper articles from 1965 have quotes from teenaged parishioners who recalled how much Father Joe had done for them. One said, "He was just always around, I don't think he ever slept." Another said, "Fr. Joe did everything". Father Laporte was diagnosed with leukemia in 1963. Rather than accept a lighter assignment where he could rest and try to be comfortable, Fr. Laporte told Cardinal Cushing, "Please leave me in South Boston, I would rather wear away working here than rust away doing nothing". For two more years Father Joe continued to work in South Boston with the kids---whether it was playing basketball, handball at the L, or hearing confessions walking on the beach---he guided them on the right path. Thousands attended his wake at Gate of Heaven

Church. He lay in state from 3pm until midnight and there was a constant stream of parishioners coming to pay their respects. His funeral Mass was standing room only with hundreds standing in the aisles. The Mass was celebrated by his friend auxiliary Bishop of Boston Most Reverend Jeremiah Minihan.

Ask the Globe

The Boston Globe, September 5, 1973

Question: Father Laporte was a native of Haverhill and I understand that somewhere in the city of Boston a statue of him has been erected. Can you tell me where it is and why he was so honored?

C.L.

Haverhill, MA

Answer: "Father Joe" Laporte was one of the most loved priests in South Boston history. A young athletic man, he was a friend, counselor, disciplinarian, confidant and adviser to hundreds of South Boston youth. In six short years as a Southie priest, he became a living legend, bringing the church to the streets, the gyms and teenage centers of Southie. He died of leukemia in 1965 at the age of 32.

The young men and women who were his friends conducted a door-to-door campaign to pay for the statue, now located directly across the street from the L. Street bath house on Day boulevard South Boston.

EULOGY

The following is a copy of the eulogy given at the funeral Mass by Father John C. Walsh, a classmate of Father Joe's at Saint John's Seminary. It was provided to the author by Richard Rouse, whose brother, Father Paul Rouse, ordained in 1967 and subsequently was assigned at Gate of Heaven, and recently died. The Rouse family were parishioners at Gate of Heaven and knew Fr. Laporte for the short time he was assigned there. I thank Richard for finding this and sending it along so it could be included in this memoir.

EULOGY FOR FATHER LAPORTE
Delivered at Gate of Heaven Church, March 17, 1965
By Father John C. Walsh

The one love that characterized the whole life of Father Laporte was his tremendous love for the priesthood. From his earliest years he showed this love and started on the road to the priesthood after graduation from St. James High School in Haverhill. During his seminary years Father Laporte showed the same characteristics that were to make his priesthood so successful---his friendliness and kindness. He knew everyone and went out of his way to welcome the new men and gave his friendship, not just to a few close associates, but to all. His years in the seminary were not easy ones as far as studies were concerned for he would readily admit that he was no brain, and he would say, "I spent three years in the minor seminary instead of two to prove it." But there was nothing that with God's help would keep him from the priesthood and he looked forward to ordination and to his work. Even before his first assignment at St. Monica's, he knew South Boston and loved her people. While out teaching Christian Doctrine at St. Peter and Paul's as a seminarian, Fr Laporte used to walk around Southie and he observed with interest the progress in the construction of the new St. Monica's Church. His subsequent assignment there after ordination was received by him with joy and enthusiasm. The new priest was immediately accepted by the people of Southie as one of their own. He had a deep sense of his mission to the people that God had given him and he started to go out and know his flock. His cheery "Hi" and joyful good nature was the introduction that made him so popular and eminently effective. His spirit of friendliness was more than just his outgoing good nature – it was the result of his intense desire to show to his people the interest of Christ in them because the priest, His representative, was interested. Even during his sickest days his courtesy and kindness was outstanding and his gratitude to the nurses and the doctors was cheerful and genuine. Fr. Laporte believed strongly that if people were going to be interested in the Church, they must first feel that the church was interested in them. He played no favorites in his friendship nor did he court those who might be influential or helpful to him. If there were any favorites, they were among those who might be rejected by others, the tough kid, the drop-out from school, the juvenile delinquent. He realized how much they needed a friend and he gave himself to them, even when others might say they were hopeless. He would reply, "He's all right, there's a lot of good in him if he will use it." There are many who perhaps found no one else who had faith in them and because of Fr. Laporte will use the good that is in them. When people find a priest that they can talk to, they come to him. His cheery greeting and friendly manner where the introduction he used to invite people to see him if they had a problem. They knew he cared. His attitude was, "If the politician can be friendly to win votes why can't we be friendly to win souls." The young people especially accepted him and they loved him because he was genuine, he had no airs or pretensions, there was not a trace of insincerity in him. He said what he meant and he meant what he said. It was not just the grammar school or high school students that loved, admired and respected him, but also the young working people who are often so hard to reach. Some not knowing him too well might wonder if the term Father Joe used by them, for him, was a little too informal. The people of South Boston and his priest friends understood how much he was loved and knew the emphasis was always on the title, he was **FATHER** Joe. To the youth of South Boston, he was a real father. The priest consecrates himself to a life of celibacy in order that being free from the obligations of his own family, he might better be the common father of all the people of his parish. Fr. Laporte understood this and lived it. His people realized it and loved him for it. His concerns for his fellow priests and respect for the priesthood was tremendous. He understood that through the priesthood, people must come to know and love Christ, and that they must meet Christ in the Sacraments and use the Sacraments to live a Christian life. He tried in every way to show the kindness and love of Christ to them hoping that through him they might find Christ. In the confessional, he was extremely kind and gentle, but still firm and honest with the penitent. The young people especially flocked to his confessional and sought his advice. For in him they found the understanding and love of Christ. He pulled no punches with them, nor did he minimize their obligations. He set high ideals and standards for them, asked them to follow them, but also understood that sometimes they might fall. Like Christ, he knew what was in man. Two years ago, when Fr. Laporte found out how seriously sick he was, he resolved not to change, but to use the time left him by Almighty God in the best way possible. He completely rejected any idea of saving himself and gave himself even more completely to his work. His anxiety or physical weakness was never reflected in his outward behavior and he told the cardinal, "Please leave me in South Boston, I would rather wear away than rust away doing nothing." So, Fr. Laporte came to live at Gate of Heaven and was given the wider assignment of working with all the youth of South Boston. He continued his winning ways and the convert work that he had initiated at St. Monica's prospered. He really didn't feel up to having another Mission for Young people, but he felt it was necessary, and he gave it again with the same outstanding success. He could feel himself slowing down, but he wouldn't give in to it. "I want to be available when people want me", he said. Christ said that the priest is the salt of the earth, and Fr. Laporte realized that salt is not good if it isn't available, and so he was there if anyone wanted him. He understood that salt belongs on the table, where it can be easily reached. Fr. Laporte appreciated the many small kindnesses and expressions of gratitude that were shown to him from time to time, and he was tremendously pleased by the testimonial dinner given him at Blinstub's last year. He was pleased because he felt it would show others how good our young people really are, for he felt people only hear bad things about them. For the priests close to him it was a wonderful tribute to his high ideals of the priesthood, and we appreciated the strength and courage it gave him to carry on his work despite the growing deadliness of his sickness, for his children had shown for all to see how much they appreciated their Father in Christ. When the time came that he had to enter the hospital again, he was well aware of the seriousness of his condition and again he asked the prayers of all his friends and especially the sisters. What faith he had in prayer! But he realized that being a priest meant being another Christ, and that if Christ would ask from him the sacrifice of his life as a victim for his people, then he was willing to accept this cross in imitation of his Master. As he lived his life every day being available for his people that they might have the grace of Christ through Him and his advice, now he made himself available for them as a victim for their sins; to win the greater grace for them by his suffering and death. With Christ, his Master, he became both priest and victim. And it was the many, many prayers of his people that gave him the courage to accept this cross willingly and carry it joyfully in order to win more grace for his people. Our prayers were answered---but in God's way, not ours. The great Cure of Ars, St. John Vianney, patron of all priests said, "The cross is the gift God gives friends. For they are the ones who love Him enough to carry it." During his last hours, knowing that his condition was critical, he dismissed the assurances of a quick recovery saying, "I don't want to talk nonsense," and spoke of the good that he hoped his sufferings might bring. He prayed that those who did not have the grace to accept his advice during his life might find greater meaning in his words in death. He prayed for those who had vocations to the priesthood and sisterhood, that they might fulfill God's will. He prayed for his fellow priests, especially his classmates. He asked for the grace for his family to accept God's will. He spoke warmly of the many people who were praying for him, and how much he appreciated it, especially the Sisters. He prayed for all those who were his penitents in confession, that they might continue in God's grace. He was a Shepherd of his flock on the sick bed, just as when he was well. I would like to propose that we erect a memorial to Fr. Laporte---the only one that he would appreciate. The memorial must be a spiritual one that only his spiritual children could build for him. You young men and young women whom he loved so much— dedicate yourselves to Christ. Live as good Catholics, faithful to the example and advice he has given you. Keep up the reception of the Sacraments frequently and live in your lives what he has taught you. Fulfill the graces of your vocations in life by doing God's will. Only then will you and your memorial be worthy of him. Fellow priests, let us try to imitate his sincerity, kindness and availability, giving ourselves completely to the work of the priesthood as he did. To his mother and family, we offer our deep sympathy and assurance of our continued prayers. Knowing Mrs. Laporte, her goodness and faith, we can understand where Fr. Laporte got his kindness and love of God. It is our prayer that Mary, the Mother of priests, will watch over and console her. Fr Laporte has attained his goal — I can picture no other scene then our Heavenly Father welcoming with outstretched arms His priestly son, Father Joseph Laporte, with the words: "THIS IS MY BELOVED SON IN WHOM I AM WELL PLEASED."

PICTURES

Father Laporte from boyhood to manhood

Family day at the beach
l-r: Joe's mother, Joe, Joe's father and Norma

Father Laporte and altar boys at St. Monica's

Southie Will Never Forget You

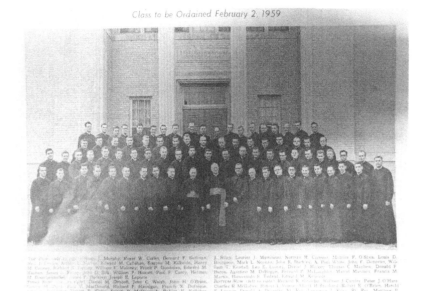

Class to be Ordained February 2, 1959

Father Laporte's Seminary Class, 1959

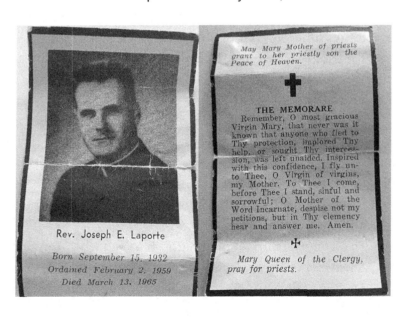

Rev. Joseph E. Laporte

Born September 15, 1932
Ordained February 2, 1959
Died March 13, 1965

May Mary Mother of priests
grant to her priestly son the
Peace of Heaven.

✝

THE MEMORARE

Remember, O most gracious
Virgin Mary, that never was it
known that anyone who fled to
Thy protection, implored Thy
help, or sought Thy interces-
sion, was left unaided. Inspired
with this confidence, I fly un-
to Thee, O Virgin of virgins,
my Mother. To Thee I come,
before Thee I stand, sinful and
sorrowful; O Mother of the
Word Incarnate, despise not my
petitions, but in Thy clemency
hear and answer me. Amen.

✠

Mary Queen of the Clergy,
pray for priests.

ACKNOWLEDGEMENTS

To Joanne Derrah, my classmate from South Boston High School, Class of 1968. Joanne spoke to me at our 50th Class reunion about her brother, Bob who knew Father Laporte and put me in touch with the other five contributors.

To the contributors, Bob Derrah, John Simpson, Frannie Madden, Joe Sheppeck, John O'Connor and Jack Hurley who shared their memories of Father Laporte and described their social contact with him.

To Mary Bulger, wife of Senate President William Bulger, who's support in the early days of this book project was unrelenting until her untimely death.

To Norma Williams Reilly and Humphrey Williams, both first cousins of Father Joe who agreed to be interviewed for this book. I thank them for their trust in this project and providing Father Joe's early life for the reader.

To Thomas P. Lester, Director, Archive and Library for the Archdiocese of Boston who I thank for all your support and assistance during these many years.

To Richard Rouse for providing the copy of the Eulogy read by Rev. John Walsh at Father Joe's funeral Mass. Rich's brother, Rev. Paul Rouse, recently deceased was a priest at Gate of Heaven after Father Joe's death. He had kept this copy and Richard gave it to me for this book, which I am eternally grateful.

To Timmy Burke of South Boston who provided assistance in making contacts with the Archdiocese of Boston.

To Rev. Bill Murphy, at Boston College who provided

Southie Will Never Forget You

assistance, thank you so much Father.

To Jake Manning, Author of, "One Nation Inside The Bricks," who provided his knowledge and support during the writing of the book. I will never forget all your help Jake.

To Boston Public Library's Research Specialists, John J. Devine Jr and Chris Glass whose help and patience enabled the finding of historic newspaper articles about Father Laporte.

I would like to pay special regards to the following newspapers for their reporting about Father Laporte:

The South Boston Tribune

The Boston Globe

The Record American

To The Eagle Tribune (North of Boston Media Group), its Editor Alexandra Nicolas and Reporter Mike LaBella thank you.

Especially want to thank Bill Brett, an award- winning photojournalist during his long career for, The Boston Globe for allowing his photograph of the Father Laporte Statue dated April 22, 1968.

To Joe Casper owner of Casper Funeral & Cremation Services, South Boston, MA. The quote, "The Gift of Love is Giving Love to Others," was his idea. Thank you Joe.

To Mike and Sue Keenan whose love, prayers and support went from my early ideas about this project right up to the completion of this book.

To Josie Zeman who edited this manuscript, I am eternally grateful for your support.

To Ray Charbonneau of Y42K Publishing Services, thank you Ray for all your technical assistance.

ABOUT THE AUTHOR

W. Thomas Stafford was born in Boston, MA and raised in South Boston. He graduated from South Boston High School class of 1968. After high school he enlisted in the United States Marine Corps and was honorably discharged in 1971. He attended Rutgers University, New Brunswick, NJ and earned a bachelor's degree in Criminal Justice. Mr. Stafford spent his career in law enforcement in the State of New Jersey. He and his wife Emma have raised four daughters and have six grandchildren.

Made in United States
North Haven, CT
02 December 2022

27707944R00085